MW00567764

McDonnell Dougla
F/A-18 Hornet

A Photo Chronicle

Bill Holder and Mike Wallace

Foreward by:
Major Martin Rollinger, USMC
F/A-18 Pilot

Schiffer Military/Aviation History
Atglen, PA

Acknowledgments

The authors are indebted to the following for their assistance in this book:

Daryl Stephenson, McDonnell Douglas Aerospace

Major Martin Rollinger, USMC

Bobby Mixon, ASC Office of Public Affairs

Aeronautical Systems Center History Office

Public Affairs Office, Arnold Engineering Development Center

Book Design by Ian Robertson.

Printed in China.
ISBN: 0-7643-0243-4

We are interested in hearing from authors with book ideas on related topics.

Published by Schiffer Publishing Ltd.
77 Lower Valley Road
Atglen, PA 19310
Phone: (610) 593-1777
FAX: (610) 593-2002
E-mail: schifferbk@aol.com
Please write for a free catalog.
This book may be purchased from the publisher.
Please include $2.95 postage.
Try your bookstore first.

Table of Contents

Foreword

The F/A-18 is the most versatile fighter in use today. The aircraft can be loaded with a variety of ordnance allowing the Hornet to perform several different missions on any given flight. Flights over Bosnia included AMRAAM and Sidewinder air-to-air missiles, HARM missiles for suppression of enemy air defenses, laser guided bombs, both laser and infrared guided Maverick missiles, and five inch rockets for attacking ground targets. Hornet drivers are trained for anti-air warfare, close air support, deep air strikes, electronic combat, and as forward air controllers.

The F/A-18 is easy to fly and has outstanding flying qualities, freeing the pilot to devote 90 percent attention to the weapons systems. Its pilots are provided with a tremendous amount of information in an easily-absorbable format. F/A-18 pilots have the ability to see through the night with their radar, two FLIR devices, and through the use of night vision goggles. Navigation is simple and precise using the Digital Moving Map display, INS, and GPS.

As computer technology has advanced so has the Hornet's lethality. During the two decades that the F/A-18 has been flying, its two mission computers have been upgraded several times increasing their memory and speed. As the F/A-18C/D versions gradually attain their full potential, the F/A-18E/F is being test flown. In addition to being able to fly farther, remain airborne longer, and carry more ordnance, the new Hornet will have more internal space, cooling, and electric power to support even more advanced avionics allowing for another two decades of growth.

Major Martin Rollinger, USMC
F/A-18 Pilot

OPPOSITE: Also built for US Marine Corps use, this is the first pre-production Marine Hornet F/A-18A sitting on the tarmac at the St. Louis company facility in November 1978. (McDonnell Douglas Photo)

Chapter 1:
Introduction

Meet the F/A-18 Hornet, a magnificent fighter-bomber that could prove to be the best Navy/Marine fighter/attack aircraft in history. Like many of the famous fighters of the past, this model too has been modified several times, the last version (the E/F) being a very extensive redesign. Before the program is over, there could be more upgrades.

This book will address all aspects of the aircraft's development program, its modifications, foreign sales, combat

Built for carrier use, sea testing was a big portion of the initial F/A-18 flight testing. Shown here is an F/A-18A Pre-Production aircraft shown on the USS Carl Vinson in March 1982. (McDonnell Douglas Photo)

The predecessor of the F/A-18 was the Northrop YF-17 which was the loser in the USAF Lightweight Fighter Competition to the General Dynamics YF-16. (USAF Photo)

The greatest Hornet of them all-The Super Hornet or F/A-18E/F in this artists concept will be the mainstay of the Navy fleet until well into the next century. (McDonnell Douglas Photo)

The second generation Hornet is typified by this C version shown carrying a laser-guided bomb, a FLIR IR system, laser designator, and various air-to-air missiles. (McDonnell Douglas Photo)

The versatile, multi-mission Hornet is easily fitted for air-to-surface missions (foreground with four Mk-84 bombs) and air-to-air missions (Background with six AIM-9 missiles). (McDonnell Douglas Photo)

record, use with the Blue Angels, involvement in test programs, and its possible future uses.

The Hornet came about in the strangest of ways, actually first being a loser in a head-to-head competition with the F-16 for the Air Force Lightweight Fighter competition. But the Navy saw its potential, and the plane would be adapted for that service. It proved to be an excellent decision.

There have actually been three generations of Hornets, with both a single and two-seat version of each. The A and B versions were first, followed by the C and D versions in the 1980s. In the 1990s, the third version-the E/F configuration which was again the winner after the AX and A-12 programs were canceled.

The Hornet has been on the combat front line on several occasions, with the biggest exposure coming from its performance in Operation Desert Storm.

A number of foreign countries have bought the Hornet, with Canada and Australia being the largest users. Undoubtedly, there will be more foreign buyers through the rest of the 1990s.

The Hornet has already seen considerable combat. Capable of carrying ten AIM-120 advanced missiles, the F/A-18 is ready for any threat well into the future. (McDonnell Douglas Photo)

Not surprisingly, the Hornet has attracted the attention of many of the free world's air forces. Here, for example, is an artist's concept of a Swiss-configured F/A-18. (McDonnell Douglas Photo)

This unique camera angle shows the US Navy aerial demonstration team, The Blue Angels, in one their many tight formations, upside-down. (US Navy Photo)

The Navy has always used its top fighter to fly with the Blue Angels, so it wasn't surprising when the Hornet was selected for the top team's aircraft.

There has also been a number of F/A-18s used in testbed configurations. The most famous of these Hornets is the so-called HARV test vehicle that has increased fighter maneuverability technology.

The story of the Hornet is far from over, and most likely, could stretch for several decades into the next century. The reason is simple. This plane is rated by many as one of the best, if not the best, fighter/attack aircraft in the world.

So here's the story of the Hornet. It's going to be a great trip, just ask any pilot who's flown it.

NASA has incorporated a number early F/A-18s into its test fleet, one of which is shown here. (NASA Photo)

Chapter 2:
Design, Development and Production

The Air Force called it 'prototyping' where two aircraft (fighters in this case) were constructed and then actually flown against each other.

It wasn't a battle of some paper mockups, but the real items attempting the same maneuvers and missions, to see which plane would come out best. The attempt was made to simulate actual missions that would be encountered in operational service.

The planes were wrung out to examine where components might fail, to see if there were deficiencies in such ar-

The YF-17 was characterized by its canted twin tails and long strake continuing the leading edge of the wing reaching to the front of the cockpit. (USAF Photo)

The YF-17, which was Northrop's entry in the USAF's Lightweight Fighter Competition, eventually evolved into the F/A-18. The Navy would later choose the YF-17 because of its two-engine configuration. The competition took place in the early 1970s. (USAF Photo)

eas as maneuverability or performance. That was the test that faced the YF-16 and YF-17 fighters in the early 1970s in the Air Force Lightweight Fighter competition.

Though the two planes were quite different in design, both were attempting to accomplish the same mission. Both General Dynamics' YF-16 and Northrop with the F-17 had some strong points going for them. The plan was that the Navy might also take the winning design and incorporate the plane into its service. That, of course, didn't happen.

The idea of using the same aircraft in both services has the attractive idea of economy with only one aircraft development required. Such an effort was attempted with the F-111 fighter-bomber, where there was an F-111A (the Air Force version) and the Navy F-111B. The redesign necessary for the Navy version to operate in a carrier environment caused it to eventually fall by the wayside.

With the F-4 Phantom, though, it was sort of a 'force fit' in making it a two-service fighter. Originally a Navy bird, the Air Force was told to adopt the fighter into its inventory. Initially, the Air Force called the plane the F-110 from its own numbering system. But eventually, it too was forced to call it the F-4. The plane would prove that the concept could work.

Department of Defense officials hoped that the same success could be realized with the winner of the Lightweight Fighter program, but as is well known, that didn't happen.

The biggest difference in the models was that the YF-16 was a single-engine plane while the YF-17 carried a pair of engines. The former design was the preference of the Air Force, while the Navy preferred the multi-engine design.

There were actually two YF-17 prototypes built: 72-01569 and 72-01570, at Northrop's Hawthorne, California facility.

The winning USAF Lightweight Fighter Competition entry was the General Dynamics YF-16 which would be built by the thousands as the F-16 Fighting Falcon in the years to follow. (USAF Photo)

An early Northrop artist's concept shows some differences in the way the aircraft finally evolved. The canted rear tails are further forward on the fuselage with a sharper pointed nose. (Northrop Photo)

The F-111 was an aircraft that some defense officials wanted for both services. The F-111B was to be the Navy version, but excess weight and other problems prevented its Naval use. (USAF Photo)

The first flights of the prototypes took place in April and August of 1974. Whereas the YF-16 got most of the publicity, it must be noted that the YF-17 was the first jet-powered US aircraft to exceed Mach 1 in level flight without an afterburner. That monumental accomplishment took place on June 11, 1974.

Northrop felt confident with its design since it was a modification of the proven F-5 and T-38, both USAF aircraft. Northrop at the time was also looking for a successor to both planes, and had come up with the P-530 Cobra design. hen the Lightweight Fighter Competition came along, the company was ready with a Cobra modification with the company name of P-600, and what the Air Force called the YF-17.

The pilots who composed the Lightweight Fighter Test Force were from both the Air Force and the contractors. The contractor teams flew their own aircraft, while the Air Force pilots flew the both models an equal number of times. Both prototypes were also flown against F-4E operational fighters of the Tactical Air Command(TAC).

Long a participant in the development of USAF fighters, the Arnold Engineering Development Center(AEDC) in Tullahoma, TN is shown here wind tunnel testing a YF-17 model in a 1974 test. (USAF Photo)

Suspended in a 1973 weight balance test, this YF-17 carries a pair of Sidewinder Missiles on its wing tips. (USAF Photo)

USAF investigated several different paint schemes for the YF-17 as shown here. (USAF Photo)

The first YF-17 prototype is shown here in an early company photo. (Northrop Photo)

A low front angle shows the sleek lines of the YF-17. But as is the case with most fighters entering the inventory, the F/A-18 is bulkier but still shows the clean curves of that early prototype. (Northrop Photo)

During the test program, the operational capability of both aircraft was tested with air-to-air and air-to-ground missions.

The test pilots also accomplished target practice on towed targets, and did ground strafing. A number of AIM-9 Sidewinder missiles were launched off each aircraft type at both subsonic and supersonic velocities.

Then in January 1975, the flight testing was over and it was nail-biting time for the contractors and the tough decision for the Air Force evaluators to make. On the 13th, then-Secretary of the Air Force John L. McLucas made the announcement that the YF-16 had been picked over the YF-17 and that production of the F-16 would soon commence. The Secretary stated that the planes were very close in performance in many of the missions, but that the YF-16 had a cleaner design and lower drag.

Almost immediately after the disappointing announcement, Northrop teamed with McDonnell-Douglas and began promoting the F-17 as a strictly-Navy fighter. It was felt that the plane could still fulfill the requirements set forth by the

F/A-18 Milestones

Date	Event
1971	U.S Navy becomes concerned with cost of F-14
April 1972	Lightweight Fighter prototype program (YF-16, YF-17) started
1973	U.S. Navy studies low-cost versions and compares them with navalized F-15 versions and improved F-4s
April 1974	DoD accepts proposal from the U.S. Navy to study a low-cost lightweight multi-mission fighter, VFAX
June 1974	USN approaches manufacturers to submit critiques and concepts; USN has responses from six manufacturers
9 June 1974	First flight of YF-17
28 August 1974	Congress terminates VFAX concept; changed to NCAF program—Navy issues operational requirement for a new multi-mission aircraft
Fall 1974	Navy is directed to limit its competition to YF-16 (General Dynamics) and YF-17 (Northrop) derivatives
12 October 1974	Requests for quotation sent out to industry
October 1974	Northrop teamed with McDonnell
December 1974	McDonnell and LTV respond with preliminary technical proposals
December-January 1975	McDonnell and LTV furnish additional data
15-16 January 1975	Navy Source Selection officials meet and advise LTV and McDonnell on the shortcomings of their proposals
January-February-March 1975	Contractors submit revised proposals
28 April 1975	Source Selection Authority selects McDonnell Model 267
2 May 1975	Public announcement of selection; initial short-term contract of $4.4 million to McDonnell Douglas/ Northrop and $2.2 to GE
9 May 1975	LTV files formal bid of protest with GAO
1 October 1974	GAO and House of Representatives uphold procurement decision; reject LTV's protest
21 November 1975	Full-scale development contract to General Electric for F404-GE-400 engine
December 1975	DSARC 11
22 January 1976(a) (FSD start)	Full-scale development contract with McDonnell Douglas for 11 R&D aircraft

McDonnell Douglas Test Pilot Jack Krings emerges from the cockpit after the first flight of the F/A-18 in November 1978. (McDonnell Douglas Photo)

As is McDonnell Douglas's custom, prototype aircraft are rolled out in front of the company sign. Here is the unpainted F/A-18 prototype so displayed. (McDonnell Douglas Photo)

Navy with its VFAX(Fighter Attack Experimental) program. A competitive model was proposed by General Dynamics/ Ling-Temco-Vought.

The fact that the basic design, manifested in the YF-17, had already flown certainly had to be a major influence in the decision. The decision was made on May 2, 1975. The USAF Lightweight Fighter loser was now the winning Navy F/A-18.

The goal of the F/A-18 was to eventually replace two operational fighters—the A-7 Corsair and the dominant F-4 Phantom—both of which had served admirably for many years. Notice that the A (for attack) and the F(for fighter) were both incorporated in the F/A-18's title.

Granted, McDonnell-Douglas and Northrop had a great start on the F/A-18 with an already-flying prototype of sorts with the YF-17, but that model would be a long way from the final F/A-18 configuration. There would be many changes made because it would become a true Navy aircraft, along with the expected growth that would occur during the research process.

One of the most prominent changes was a more substantial landing gear required for carrier operations. The additional structural beefing up of the fuselage also considerably increased the F/A-18's weight over the YF-17. It was a jump of some five tons, resulting in quite a different beast. The new engines would provide about a thousand pounds more thrust each over the YF-17 value.

Also, there were also the squared-off fin tips and reshaped Leading Edge Extension(LEX). The F/A-18 carried a larger

nose profile to accommodate the APG-65 radar system and larger landing gear arrangement.

It was specified from the very beginning of the program that the F/A-18 Hornet had to be compatible with the AIM-7F

The initial Hornet name, as shown here on the prototype, carried a unique F-18 A-18 designation, which would later be shortened to F/A-18. Also notice the Navy insignia and Hornet logo. (McDonnell Douglas Photo)

The first F/A-18 prototype is taxiing at McDonnell Douglas in 1978. Although not designed specifically to be stealthy, the Hornet displays small a radar cross section when approaching head-on. (McDonnell Douglas Photo)

Sparrow which required all-weather avionics and a high-tech fire control system. There was also a requirement for increased endurance, thus indicating more fuel capacity, with the final result necessitating the aforementioned more powerful engines than were in the prototype. Since the Hornet would only have a single pilot in most of its versions, initial attention was paid to reducing the pilot work load. To that end, the requirement for a so-called Hands On Throttle and Stick (HOTAS) cockpit was adopted.

Adding such requirements, of course, added significantly to the cost of the F/A-18, but recall that the new plane was being asked to actually perform the missions of the two planes it was replacing.

The Navy at the time was hoping that a long production run(which has actually happened) would reduce the cost of the plane. Another goal of the Navy at the time was to reduce the number of aircraft types in the fleet, which the F/A-18 has accomplished well through its years of operational service stretch into the mid-1990s.

Other requirements for the new plane were listed by Vice Admiral W. D. Houser who was the then-Deputy Chief of Naval Operations(Air Warfare) who indicated that the F-18 (obviously) had to be carrier-compatible and serve as a complement to the already existing F-14 aircraft, have lower operating costs than the F-14, and also on occasion be able to be employed in a reconnaissance mission scenario.

This interesting angle of the first F/A-18 clearly shows its twin engines and clean aerodynamic design. It's a look that wouldn't basically change through the next two evolutions of the Hornet. (McDonnell Douglas Photo)

Since both the Marines and Navy would be using the Hornet, each service's name was on each test plane. Navy identification was on port(left) side while the Marine name was carried on the starboard(right) side. This particular aircraft was the second F/A-18 test plane. (McDonnell Douglas Photo)

Although the actual selection of the McDonnell-Douglas/Northrop consortium was pronounced the winner in May 1975, it wouldn't be until late January l976 that the official paperwork would be signed. That initial contract called for the fabrication of 11 full scale development(FSD) models. The breakout on the numbers saw nine of the planes being the single-seat version(coined F-18As) while the two-seat versions had the TF-18A designation.

With most test programs, it would have been necessary to wait until the first FSD aircraft was ready before the flight testing could begin. Not the case here as the YF-17 aircraft were pushed into test service at several Navy test ranges.

Commander Larry Blose was one of the early test pilots that exercised the YF-17 prototypes at the Edwards Test Fa-

cility in the Mojave Desert. Blose was impressed with the F-18 concept from the beginning.

"It's the most impressive aircraft I've ever flown," he explained. "The performance, rate of climb, maneuverability and superb flying qualities make it an aircraft that is extremely easy to fly and one that can easily defeat any other aircraft in air combat...After only two flights, I knew that I could comfortably take the aircraft to the extremes of the flight envelope and land aboard a carrier safely."

The FSD birds were painted up in proud fashion with macho detailing on the body strakes and on the leading edge of the twin vertical stabilizers. The word 'Hornet' was blocked out on the center fuselage of a number of the aircraft. There

A portion of the flight test program was inflight refueling, the Number One prototype shown here performing this function in March 1979. (McDonnell Douglas Photo)

The third F/A-18 is shown in a landing mode with its huge trailing edge flaps deployed in June 1979. (McDonnell Douglas Photo)

were FSD models that carried the Navy emblem while others were denoted as Marine aircraft.

With the awarding of the F/A-18 contract, an interesting confrontation took place when the Navy proposed a land-based version of the F/A-18, a model which would be called the F-18L.

The plane was proposed as a competitor to that good old adversary—the F-16.

Of course, the F-18L never came to pass-certainly to the relief of General Dynamics, prime F-16 contractor-but it certainly kept things interesting for awhile during the mid-1970s.

The YF-17 prototype, in Navy garb, was flown at the Farnborough Air Show in England to actually promote the F-18L concept. The YF-17 designation on the tail was gone replaced by an American flag. This appearance was the first time the model had been flown outside the United States.

One of the main reasons the Navy selected the Hornet was its dependability and ease of maintenance. Also, the Hornet presented a future growth potential. (McDonnell Douglas Photo)

During initial sea trails in 1982 aboard the USS Carl Vinson, the F/A-18 had to prove its compatibility with carrier landing and take-offs. (McDonnell Douglas Photos)

There were significant differences between the F/A-18 and proposed land-based version, although the General Electric F404 engines were standard in both designs. Even with the differences, there was still up to 90 percent commonality of parts.

The first flight of an FSD Hornet wouldn't actually take place until November 1978. It was behind the intended schedule, but fortunately, there were no glitches in this important flight. Patuxent River Naval Air Station would be the site for the extensive flight testing program to follow. To work closely

Space is a critical commodity aboard a carrier. As such, all aircraft must have a folding-wing capability. This photo shows the Number Three test plane in that configuration. (McDonnell Douglas Photo)

Everything that happens on a carrier deck is generally frantic and potentially dangerous. This photo was obviously shot during a relaxed moment during carrier suitability testing. (McDonnell Douglas Photo)

with the Navy, a sizable contingent of McDonnell-Douglas personnel were transferred to the location. The 11 FSD birds would accomplish the majority of the flying goals, but near the end of the program, a number of early 'pilot-production' Hornets would also be integrated into the tests.

With carrier operations being an important part of the F/A-18 operational scenario, it wasn't surprising that the Navy/contractor team vigorously investigated the Hornet in that strenuous environment. To that end, the FSD plane number 3 was exercised with some 70 catapult launches and 120 arrested landings(all simulated) at the Patuxent so-called 'concrete aircraft carrier.'

Another important part of the testing was to ensure the compatibility between the Hornet and USAF inflight refueling transports. Some testing involved tests with the KC-10 refueling aircraft.

In 1979, it was finally time to take one of the research F/A-18s to sea; the carrier chosen was the USS America which tested the Hornet in an actual operational environment. The

testing involved launch and recovery performance, as well as how the plane could be supported on and below deck.

As is always the case with any new aircraft design, there would be some changes incorporated into the basic F/A-18 as a result of testing. For the Hornet, there was the elimination of the leading edge slots that produced unacceptable drag, along with the discarding of the notches in the wings and vertical tail surfaces.

Compatibility with existing ordnance was a prime part of the test program with just about every type and combination of bombs, missiles, and external fuel tanks being tested. There was also extensive testing accomplished with the Hornet's awesome 20mm Vulcan nose-mounted cannon.

The Navy turned to the Air Force for one of the Hornet's test goals with climatic testing at Eglin Air Force Base, Florida. These tests subjected the Hornet to temperatures from -65 degrees to +125 degrees and winds up to 100 miles per hour.

During the test program, there were a couple of unfortunate accidents. At the 1980 Farnborough Air Show, one of

Later test aircraft were adorned with bright red detailing as demonstrated by Number Six during testing at the Patuxent River test facility in 1978. (McDonnell Douglas Photo)

the FSD Hornets had an in-flight engine explosion and crashed. Then, only a month later, one of the pilot production planes crashed in Chesapeake Bay, at a time when the first operational squadron was being established. The latter accident brought forth a vigorous investigation which resulted in the installation of a spin-recovery switch to override the onboard computer and initiate corrective maneuvers.

This F/A-18D was the thousandth Hornet produced, this photo being taken in 1991. As of mid-1996, the Hornet(including foreign Hornets) fleet had flown over 4.7 million hours of flight time. (McDonnell Douglas Photo)

The flowing lines of the F/A-18C can be seen from this view in the contractor's plant during final assembly. Note the wingtips are in the space-saving storage configuration. (McDonnell Douglas Photo)

Chapter 3:
Parts and Pieces

Compared to the sharp, needle-like lines of its forerunner, the YF-17, the F/A-18 is rather unremarkable in its looks. This "ordinariness" is emphasized by the dull, gray Navy paint scheme. However, its performance and features belie the look of the plane.

The Hornet features fly-by-wire controls with mechanical back-ups, twin turbofan engines, and swept wings constructed of light alloy and graphite composite materials (during a test, an F/A-18's wing inner spar was completely destroyed by a

Looking forward, a close-up view of the nose wheel landing gear assembly. Note the ruggedness of the design. A early test of the assembly came when the Navy hoisted a Hornet several feet into the air and dropped it onto a parking lot to test the gear. The Hornet came through unscathed. (US Navy Photo)

One of the main modes of operation for the F/A-18 was the ability to operate off a carrier. In this photo, this A version is shown preparing to land on the USS Midway. Note the deployed arresting hook which will engage cables across the deck. (US Navy Photo)

The characteristic wing strakes are clearly visible in this photo. Also note the nose wheel landing gear assembly which contains the joining mechanism to mate the plane with the deck mounted catapult. (US Navy Photo)

20mm cannon round and the wing was still able to bear loads). Long strakes extend to the front of the cockpit and the wings' leading and trailing edge flaps are computer-controlled—the leading edge flaps aid in the Hornet's magnificent maneuverability and can extend a maximum of 30 degrees.

The F/A-18's twin tails are placed forward between the trailing edge of the wing and the leading edge of the vertical tail; this placement minimizes the airflow drag around the fuselage. The vertical tails, likewise, offset drag-producing vortices developing from the wings' leading edges.

Other external features of the Hornet include: the flare/chaff dispenser located beneath the intake duct; the superb, high-visibility canopy which affords the pilot an all-around view (the view aft is especially good and is enhanced by rear-view mirrors); the tiny ultra-high frequency/identification friend-or-foe (IFF) antenna a few feet behind the cockpit canopy; and assorted "bumps" housing various antennas and fuel dump nozzles on the upper parts of the vertical tails. The Hornet has formation lights: horizontal on either side of the forward fuselage and vertical on the outsides of the vertical tails. Under the portside forward fuselage formation light is the radar

OPPOSITE: This photo shows the details of the canopy in its open position. The large size of this aircraft is illustrated by the size of the ground crewman. Also, note the low stance of the Hornet with the centerline fuel tank almost touching the ground. (McDonnell Douglas Photo)

This view of an F/A-18C is looking front-to-rear underneath the fuselage. Visible is the nose wheel landing gear assembly with its rugged shock-absorbing system. Note the large landing light. (Bill Holder Photo)

Note the higher seat position of the rear crewman of this D version for visibility purposes. The Navy two-seat versions are normally used in a training role. (McDonnell Douglas Photo)

warning receiver antenna. Further aft are an angle-of-attack sensor vane and static pitot probe.

The nose of the Hornet is a radome, hinged to starboard, which encloses the radar scanner and tracking mechanism. The scanner is linked to the multimode radar (most F/A-18s are equipped with the very reliable and combat-proven Hughes APG-65 radar; later model Cs and Ds are fitted with the Hughes APG-73, which has not only much more capability in terms of memory and higher throughput speed but also

The Hornet's unique fuselage shaping is evident from this rear perspective. Notice the aerodynamic tail-off behind the cockpit and the smoothing for the engine nacelles. (McDonnell Douglas Photo)

Unlike the USAF F-15, the Hornet's rear vertical tails are canted slightly outward. Constructed of space-age composite material, the structures are extremely thin, but strong, and create minimal drag in flight. (McDonnell Douglas Photo)

The Hornet's drag brake, shown here deployed on an early prototype, is a feature on all A-D Hornets. Its shape conforms to the shape of the rear fuselage and engine nacelles. (McDonnell Douglas Photo)

Main gear retraction has the wheels being pulled inward and upward into the mid-fuselage. Then, the doors close around them. (McDonnell Douglas Photo)

growth potential). Both types of radar are modular with built-in test equipment which speeds up maintenance and repair.

The radar system gives the pilot automatic search, detection and tracking of aerial targets. "Tracking" translates into automatic aiming of the fighter's variety of air-to-air weapons. These include the AIM-7 Sparrow, AIM-9 Sidewinder and the M61A1 20mm nose-mounted cannon.

The radar-guided AIM-7 has a range of 25 or more miles (making it beyond visual range) and attacks at more than Mach 4 speeds. Its detonation—either by impact or proximity—scatters some 2600 steel fragments giving the Sparrow a high kill probability. The Sparrow is being replaced by the AIM-120 AMRAAM (Advanced Medium Range Air-to-Air Missile) which can track and home on dissimilar targets beyond visual range. Like the Sparrow, the AMRAAM is carried on outboard wing and nacelle stations.

A trend in late model fighter aircraft is also used by the F/A-18 of four rear control surfaces. All these control surfaces are extremely thin, yet strong, due to the use of composite and alloy materials. (Bill Holder Photo)

Details of the F/A-18A's vertical starboard tail. The rectangular strip in mid-tail is a formation light. Also note a second light in the fuselage directly above the Marine name. The lowest bump on the top of the tail is for dumping fuel with antennae located above. (Bill Holder Photo)

The pointed nose of the Hornet houses the antenna of the aircraft's main APG-65 radar which was combat-proven in Desert Storm. The openings directly above and behind the radome are for the 20mm Vulcan rotary cannon which can fire at a maximum rate of 6,000 rounds per minute. The center opening is where the rounds emerge with muzzle gas deflection being the purpose of the outer two openings. (Bill Holder Photo)

The AIM-7 Sparrow, a radar-guided air-to-air missile, has long been a standard air defense missile for both the Navy and Air Force. Early versions of this missile proved effective during Vietnam. (McDonnell Douglas Photo)

The AIM-9, some versions of which were used in Vietnam, is infra-red guided. Its seeker can guide the missile toward the image created by the friction heat of the target moving through the air (the Sidewinder's guidance system automatically filters out non-target IR sources such as the sun). The AIM-9 is used to attack shorter distance (in the area of out to 11 miles or possibly more) aircraft. It has a speed of Mach 2.5. Prior to 1984, the Hornet carried AIM-9Ls which could attack targets from any direction—not just against the rear heat source. Since 1984, the improved AIM-9M has been used.

The Hornet's Vulcan rotary cannon is loaded with 578 rounds and can be fired at a maximum rate of 6,000 rounds-per-minute! The gun-port is located directly above the radar but the pilot can fire the gun at night without being blinded by the muzzle-flash, and a deflector prevents gun gases being ingested by the engines.

On later versions of the C/D's, the APG-65 was placed by the APG-73 Radar. The new system provides much greater speed and capacity for tracking targets. It also has increased reliability and easier maintenance without any increase in size or weight. (Hughes Photo)

The Hornet is one tough fighter. This plane survived a mid-air collision with another Hornet and made it back to Naval Air Station Oceana, Virginia in 1996. Flown by Navy Lt. Commander Greg Anderson. In the impact, the plane lost its radome, radar, an access door, canopy, and a centerline fuel tank. Also, there was foreign object damage to the starboard engine. (US Navy Photo)

This Hornet releases a pair of AIM-9 Sidewinder infrared air-to-air missiles in a salvo launch. Like the Sparrow, this system also was used in Southeast Asia. This missile is relatively short range system with a range of about 11 miles. (McDonnell Douglas Photo)

This photo shows a close-up of a starboard wing-tip mounted AIM-9 Sidewinder taken during the 1989 Dayton Air Show. (John Farquhar Photo)

Two F/A-18s are shown firing Sidewinders. This missile focuses on heat images generated by the target's friction heat of the target moving through the air. It has a speed of Mach 2.5. Modern AIM-9s can attack targets from any direction, not from just a rear heat source. (McDonnell Douglas Photo)

Another joint-service missile, the AIM-120 AMRAAM is a long range air-to-air missile. The missile was incorporated for fleet use in 1993. (McDonnell Douglas Photo)

A Harpoon missile is being fired off this F/A-18D. Note the characteristic Mach Rings in the rocket engine exhaust. (McDonnell Douglas Photo)

The F/A-18 also can carry a forward-looking infra-red (FLIR) pod and laser spot tracker pod to provide extremely accurate air-to-surface capabilities. This accuracy coupled with the Hornet's ordnance-carrying capabilities make it especially deadly to surface targets.

The Hornet can carry Mark 82, 83, and 84 (500, 1000, and 2000-lb, respectively) bombs while flying at very low altitudes. The bombs feature "Snakeye" fins which slow their fall to allow the aircraft to leave the area safely. On its outboard wing stations, the F/A-18 can carry AGM-62 Walleye electro-optical-guided bombs and on all but the innermost stations the Hornet can carry 486-lb Rockeye II anti-tank bombs or 610-lb BL-755 cluster bombs. It also can carry the GBU-10E/B laser-guided bomb.

For attacking surface-to-air missile sites, the F/A-18 is capable of carrying HARM high-speed anti-radiation missiles.

How's this for a full load of AMRAAMs on this F/A-18? Eight AMRAAMS, four under each wing, and two on the fuselage give this Hornet an awesome offensive look. (McDonnell Douglas Photo)

The anti-ship mission of the Hornet is carried out by the air-to-surface Harpoon missile shown here during testing. (McDonnell Douglas Photo)

This Hornet carries the whole suite of Navy missiles. AIM-9s are located on the wingtips, with AIM-7s on the fuselage, an AMRAAM under the left wing with a Harpoon under the right. (McDonnell Douglas Photo)

A pair of Mark 83 low drag bombs are dropped from this F/A-18C. (McDonnell Douglas Photo)

It can also be fitted to carry two AGM-84 Harpoon anti-ship missiles as well as two AGM-65 Maverick air-to-surface missiles. The Hornet is capable of carrying four conventional launchers and unguided missiles and at least three kinds of practice bombs.

The F/A-18 internally carries just under 11,000 lbs of JP-5 fuel. To add to this—and give the aircraft extra range—the Hornet can carry as many as three external tanks each with a 2,200-lb fuel capacity (the extra fuel is one item which can add up to the maximum takeoff gross weight of nearly 52,000 lbs). All fuel tanks and fuel lines are self-sealing and the main tanks contain fire-retarding foam. The external tanks are mounted centerline and on inner wing weapons carriage stations. The Hornet is also air-refuelable and has a retractable refueling probe on the starboard side of the cockpit's windscreen.

Eight Mark 83 Bombs are carried on the wing pylon positions of this F/A-18C. Mark 82s, 83s, and 84s are 500, 1000, and 2000 pounds, respectively. The bombs' snakeye fins slow the fall allowing the aircraft to leave the area safely. The Hornet can mount either bombs, rocket pods, or missiles on these pylon positions. (McDonnell Douglas Photo)

Details of the port side pylon release mechanism are shown by this photo. (Bill Holder Photo)

Below and to the rear of the cockpit is the centerline fuel tank, which can be jettisoned. The Hornet can carry three of these tanks. Barely visible behind and to the left of the tank is a FLIR pod equipped with a Laser Target Designator/Ranger which enables the F/A-18 to mark a target with a laser beam and hit the target with a laser-guided bomb. (McDonnell Douglas Photo)

Twin engines form the heart of the Hornet's performance (as well as one of the bases for the U.S. Navy's choice of the then-YF-17). F/A-18As and Bs are equipped with General Electric F404-GE-400 engines each capable of 16,000 lbs of augmented thrust.

To meet Swiss-Kuwaiti time-to-climb requirements, General Electric introduced, for the F/A-18C/D, the F404-GE-402 Enhanced Performance Engine. The 402 kept the reliability and maintainability of the 400, but the specific fuel consumption was improved and the maximum augmented thrust was boosted to 17,700 lbs.

Higher thrust without afterburner has resulted in a performance capability known as "supercruise." Supercruise capability means that the F/A-18C/D can fly supersonically for relatively long periods without afterburner ("supercruise" is a design goal of the Air Force F-22 Advanced Tactical Fighter program; see Future chapter).

Note: the F/A-18E/F is powered by two F414 engines, derivative of the F404, each capable of 22,000 lbs. of thrust. Unfortunately, since the F414 has a slightly larger diameter than the F404, retrofits to the A/B/C/D are impossible. All versions of the F404 and F414 are smokeless.

The newest F/A-18, the E/F(covered in Chapter 6) carries the 20mm Vulcan gun in its nose just like its predecessors(the A-D) in the background. The E/F has an extra wing station over the earlier Hornets. A-D experience aided heavily in the design of the E/F. (McDonnell Douglas Photo)

F414-GE-400 Turbofan Engine

The business end of the GE F404 powerplant. This engine provides over 16,000 pounds of thrust. The enhanced version produces nearly 18,000 pounds. The E/F engine is a follow-on to the F404, designated the F414, it provides 22,000 pounds of thrust and has a slightly larger diameter. (McDonnell Douglas Photo)

A side view of the advanced F414-GE-400, a powerplant which will be used on the E/F, an improvement over the existing F404 versions. The F414 has a maximum thrust of 22,000 pounds with manufacturing development began in 1992. (GE Photo)

The F/A-18's wings must fold up to conserve "parking" space aboard carriers. Another carrier-specific feature is the catapult launch bar, a protrusion forward from the nosewheel landing gear assembly. This allows the aircraft to be "pulled" by the carrier's steam catapult up to about 180 knots at heavy gross weights for takeoff augmentation. The aircraft's landing gear is extremely rugged in order to withstand carrier landings which have been described as "controlled crashes." Landings are aided by lowering an arresting hook to catch one of the cables across the carrier deck. Also helping slow the Hornet for conventional landings is the large, dorsal airbrake mounted between the vertical tails.

The unforgiving nature of carrier operations clearly illustrates not only the need for significant engine power but reliability. (McDonnell Douglas Photo)

The F404-GE-402 EPE engine enables the F/A-18C to fly supersonically without afterburner. (McDonnell Douglas Photo)

Another "carrier friendly" aspect of the Hornet is the fact that almost all of the aircraft's 268 access panels can be reached by a maintenance person standing on the deck. Also, more than half of the access panels have quick release latches. These features combine to allow rapid servicing of

Like every Navy carrier aircraft, the carrier-friendly Hornet has folding wingtips because of space constraints. Also, maintenance is enhanced by the accessibility on the deck of nearly all the aircraft's 268 access panels which can be opened by personnel standing on the deck. More than half of those panels have quick release panels. (McDonnell Douglas Photo)

aircraft subsystems and avionics. The Hornet even features a retractable boarding ladder!

If the engines form the heart of the Hornet, the cockpit features make up the brain. Inside, instead of facing a massive array of gauges and knobs, the pilot looks at three cathode ray tubes onto which he can call up whatever information—such as the various radar mode displays: air scans of various distances, terrain avoidance, surface search, etc.—he needs to fly and carry out missions. There also is a head-up display (HUD) upon which navigation, attitude and other data are projected and through which the pilot can see. HUD information also includes positioning cues to aid in carrier landings. The cockpit is designed to allow the pilot to spend as much time as possible with "eyes up."

The control stick is conventionally "between the knees" and the throttle is left of the pilot, who sits in a slightly-reclined position (for greater G-force tolerance). His seat is a rocket-powered Martin-Baker SJU-5/6 ejection seat. Arresting hook control for carrier landings is to the pilot's right.

Throughout most of the F/A-18's existence, it's had a Targeting Forward Looking Infra Red (TFLIR) for night strike capabilities. Beginning in fiscal year 1990, an IR navigation sensor for night flying called NAVFLIR along with color digital moving maps and special cockpit lighting which allowed the use of night-vision goggles were installed on Lot 12 F/A-18 C/Ds. In 1993, a laser designator was added to the TFLIR

The Hornet also has to be moved on the ground which is accomplished by attaching the ground support vehicle two bar to a hard point on the wheel assembly. (John Farquhar Photo)

and in 1995 the TFLIR was upgraded to include an integral laser spot tracker. These features allow the Hornet pilot to designate a target with a laser beam, release a laser-guided weapon and leave the scene while the weapon flies itself to the designated target.

The Marine Corps is scheduled to get a reconnaissance version of the Hornet in 1998. Designated the F/A-18D (RC), this aircraft will be equipped with the Loral Advanced Tactical Airborne Reconnaissance System (ATARS) and an upgraded version of the APG-73 radar. The purpose is to satisfy the requirement for real or near-real-time reconnaissance of the battlefield. The ATARS will replace the 20mm cannon in the Hornet's nose and

provide high resolution, day-or-night imagery which can be transmitted to a ground base via a new data link. Since early 1992, the Marine F/A-18Ds have been able to accommodate the ATARS package.

The arresting hook of the F/A-18 is located below and between the engine exhaust nozzles. Without this device, landing on a carrier would be impossible. (Bill Holder Photo)

Chapter 4:
(F/A-18) A Through D

The F/A-18 Hornet is a frontline fighter aircraft for the U.S. Navy and Marine Corps. Recall that it is a craft that grew out of the U.S. Air Force Lightweight Fighter program which involved a "fly-off" competition between the prototypes: YF-16 and YF-17. The YF-16 became the F-16 and the YF-17 evolved into the F/A-18, which first flew in late 1978. The first aircraft designated F-18 began tests in November 1979.

Driving the development was the emergence of the Soviet SU(Sukhoi)-17, designated "FITTER" by the North Atlantic Treaty Organization (NATO), and the SU-19, designated "FENCER ," which was considered equivalent to U.S. F-111s. To achieve air superiority, the Navy first developed the variable-geometry-winged F-14 Tomcat and, in the mid-1970s, decided to replace all its remaining F-4 Phantoms with the F/A-18.

Used by the Navy and Marine Corps, the Hornet is an all-weather, multi-mission fighter and attack aircraft known as the nation's first strike-fighter. In its attack configuration, the F/A-18 is used for force projection, interdiction and both close and deep air support; in its fighter configuration, it's used as fighter escort and fleet defense.

F/A-18s can be changed with the flip of a switch to perform either fighter or attack roles (additionally, for attacks, the Hornet is fitted with a laser spot tracker/strike camera). This rapid reconfiguration capability makes the F/A-18 a "force multiplier" by giving an operational commander more flexibility in employing fighters in the flux of changing battle conditions.

The F/A-18 Hornet's major contractor isMcDonnell Douglas and its major subcontractor is Northrop. The F/A-18's general description includes: propulsion by two General Electric smokeless, low-bypass turborfan F404 engines each having a thrust of 16,000 or more pounds; overall length of 56 feet; height of 15 feet, three inches; and a wingspan of 40 feet, five inches. Maximum takeoff weight varies from 36, 628

The F/A-18A, a model which was first delivered in May 1980, is shown in flight over the China Lake test area in California. (US Navy Photo)

Clearly visible on these F/A-18As are their leading edge strakes which reach nearly the front of the cockpit wind screen. (McDonnell Douglas Photo)

With its two-man cockpit, the F/A-18B takes on a different look although its capabilities are almost identical to the single seat A version. The model's main purpose is that of a trainer. (McDonnell Douglas Photo)

A single-seat F/A-18C and a two-seat F/A-18D home-based at Beaufort, South Carolina fly over the mountains near the target range in Fallon, Nevada in 1993. In all, US Navy and US Marine F/A-18C/D purchases totaled 575 in mid-1996. (McDonnell Douglas Photo)

pounds for the fighter configuration to nearly 52,000 pounds for the attack configuration. The Hornet can fly at more than one-and-a-half times the speed of sound.

The F/A-18 can carry a maximum of 13,700 lbs of armament. It has one internal 20mm MK-61A1 Vulcan cannon and nine external weapons stations for the following: two wing-tip for Sidewinder heat-seeking missiles; two outboard wing for air-to-ground ordnance and for Sparrow radar-guided missiles, air-to-ground, or fuel tanks; two nacelle fuselage for two Sparrow missiles or sensor pods; one centerline for weapons, sensor pods or fuel tank. The outboard wing and nacelle stations have AMRAAM (Advanced Medium-Range Air-to-Air

Carrying both a centerline and wing-mounted fuel tanks, this F/A-18C is flying a mission over the western United States in December 1993. (McDonnell Douglas Photo)

This F/A-18C carries a laser-guided bomb on its left wing station along with a forward-looking infrared pod equipped with a laser target generator/ranger on its fuselage below and left of the center fuel tank. This pod enables the aircraft to mark a target with a laser beam which the laser guided bomb can follow to the target with pinpoint precision. (McDonnell Douglas Photo)

A Marine Corps F/A-18D practices a bombing mission over the targeting range near Naval Air Station Fallon, Nevada in June of 1993. (McDonnell Douglas Photo)

Missile) carriage capability. The Hornet can also carry Harpoon, HARM, SLAM and Maverick missiles.

The F/A-18A made its maiden flight November 18, 1978. First deliveries were made in May 1980 and, together, the U.S. Navy and Marine Corps received 409 A/Bs. Initial operational capability (IOC) was established on January 7, 1983 by a Marine Corps squadron, VMFA-314 at Marine Corps Air Station El Toro, California. The Navy's IOC took place in October 1983 with squadron VFA-113. Squadrons VFA-113 and

VFA-25 completed the first operational carrier deployment aboard the USS Constellation in August 1985.

First flight of the C version was September 3, 1987 with fleet deliveries following soon after. As of June 1996, USN/USMC F/A-18C/Ds totaled 575. Eight foreign nations either fly or have ordered the F/A-18 and there are more than 300 Hornets in service in foreign air forces. By mid-1996, the F/A-18 had flown more than 2.7 million hours.

A Navy F/A-18C carrying AIM-9 Sidewinder missiles heads out on an air police mission. The multi-mission Hornet has proved to be the most versatile fighter in the Navy's history. (McDonnell Douglas Photo)

In a formation of Hornets, a single F/A-18C leads three two-seat F/A-18Ds on a practice mission. (McDonnell Douglas Photo)

This F/A-18D carrying a Mk-82 500 pound bomb on training mission over the western US desert. (McDonnell Douglas Photo)

The Navy operates 22 active tactical squadrons of F/A-18s at Naval Air Station Cecil Field, Naval Air Station Lemoore, and Naval Air Station Atsugi, Japan. Additionally, support squadrons are based at Naval Air Station Fallon, Nevada; and Naval Air Weapons Center China Lake, California. Hornets are deployed aboard the aircraft carriers USS Constellation, USS Kitty Hawk, USS America, USS Eisenhower, USS Roosevelt, USS Nimitz, USS Kennedy, USS Washington, USS Lincoln, USS Enterprise and USS Vinson.

The F/A-18 is based in the Far East at Marine Corps Air Station Iwakuni, Japan on a forward deployment basis on a six-month rotation generally with two squadrons present at all times and a third permanently based squadron. Also, the USS Independence, deployed to Japan, is home to two squadrons.

The Marines operate 16 active tactical squadrons from Marine Corps Air Station El Toro and Naval Air Station

This D version Hornet drops a Mk-83 Low Drag bomb over a Nevada range. From Marine Unit VMFA(AW)-533, this was one plane from this unit which took top honors in the 1994 Low Country Bombing Derby at the Townsend Target Complex in Georgia. (McDonnell Douglas Photo)

This photo shows an early reconnaissance variant of the USMC F/A-18 using an early A version for the test vehicle. (McDonnell Douglas Photo)

Miramar, California as well as from Marine Corps Air Station Beaufort, South Carolina.

F/A-18A and C models are single-seat fighters while F/A-18B and D models are dual-seaters. Both Bs and Ds are used as trainers and the Marines use the D for attack, tactical air control, forward air control and reconnaissance squadrons. F/A-18Bs and Ds are as virtually indistinguishable from each other as are As and Cs; the only visual differences are of the extra "bumps" on the vertical tails of the later model C/Ds.

Block upgrades culminating in 1987 resulted in F/A-18Cs and Ds which have provisions for employing newer missiles and jamming devices against enemy ordnance. F/A-18Cs and Ds delivered since 1989 also have improved night attack capabilities. In fact all Hornets are equipped with systems for nighttime flying capabilities.

The U.S. Navy began evaluating a reconnaissance version of the F/A-18A in the Fall of 1982. The aircraft was modified with a twin sensor package replacing the 20mm cannon in the Hornet's nose. The sensors included low and medium altitude, panoramic camera systems along with a line scanner for location identification purposes. The aircraft was quickly convertible back to a fighter/attack aircraft.

The Marines began receiving the reconnaissance-configurable F/A-18D in February 1992. The two-seat aircraft's crew consists of a pilot and a sensor systems operator who manages the Advanced Tactical Airborne Reconnaissance System (ATARS). This long-range tactical reconnaissance capability will be available in 1998 and flight testing is progressing in the mid-1990s at the Naval Air Warfare Center-China Lake, California and at Naval Air Station Patuxent River, Maryland.

Reportedly, Marine Corps F/A-18Cs operating in the mid-1990s in Bosnia from VMFA251 Squadron were equipped with the ALQ-165 Airborne Self-Protection Jammer for added survivability.

As of the mid-1990s, U.S. Hornets fly in 38 tactical squadrons from air stations worldwide and from 10 aircraft carriers. Also, the Navy's Blue Angels Flight Demonstration Team uses the F/A-18 (See Chapter 8).

Chapter 5:
The Hornet in Combat

Mention combat experience for the F/A-18 and most will immediately point to its huge successes in Operation Desert Storm. But there was much more as the Hornet has been called upon a number of times.

The first flash of combat took place in 1980s when the model was called upon to support an attack on Libya. Coined

Operation El Dorado Canyon, Hornets attacked and destroyed a number of surface-to-air missile sites. Then there was Desert Storm, and what a job this aircraft did!

DESERT STORM

The big show and a time for the F/A-18 to shine, and shine it did. Navy and Marine Hornets were a part of the first strike of the war, and there till the finish.

It started on January 17, 1991, when the F/A-18s participated as a part of a coordinated attack on Iraq on the eastern front. With A-6s, the Hornets struck along the area nearest Kuwait and actually into Kuwait. It was a part of a massive three hundred plane attack which was supported by about 160 tankers.

In addition to purely offensive scenarios, the Hornet also served in an unexpected reconnaissance role. A number of F/A-18Ds proved invaluable for providing intelligence on the battlefield situation. The aircraft's forward-looking infrared FLIR system was also used in daytime operations for battlefield assessment of damage accomplished in earlier raids. These Hornets were given the nickname of 'Fast FACs'.

There were only 84 Marine Hornets(also D models) in the conflict. The Marine F/A-18s were a part of a Marine contingent which included 20 A-6 Intruders, 12 AE-6B jamming aircraft, and 19 tankers. There were also 18 Canadian Air Force Hornets in action which exhibited excellent performance in accomplishing their mission too. It was the complete Canadian contingent.

The US Navy chose the Hornet because of its carrier operations capability. Note the apparent confusion on the deck with maintenance activities, deck personnel ready to give the pilot the go-ahead, along with the ever-present high-pressure steam from the catapult. (McDonnell Douglas Photo)

A Hornet leaves the deck of the USS Constellation courtesy of a tremendous boost from the ship's catapult to boost the fighter up to 150 miles an hour. (McDonnell Douglas Photo)

Landing on a carrier has been described as a 'controlled crash' with pilot skill, a strong undercarriage, and a grappling hook to engage a cable stretched across the deck coming together to avert disaster. Shown here is a successful return to the nuclear-powered USS Enterprise of an F/A-18A (US Navy Photo)

Space is at a minimum on a carrier deck. Note the close proximity of these C versions with their folded wingtips and tails protruding over the ocean. (McDonnell Douglas Photo)

The 'F' in the F/A-18 designation was brought to light in Desert Storm particularly vividly on January 17th when, on a ground attack mission, a pair of USN Hornets were jumped by a pair of MiG-21 fighters. The Hornets pulled up, quickly did away with the bandits, and then finished their ground attack mission.

With the 190 Hornets deployed for the war, there were some 10,000 sorties flown with approximately 25,000 flight hours. In all, some 18 million pounds of ordnance was dropped during the conflict. Their efficiency was outstanding with a mission readiness of 91.5 percent and 90.4 percent mission capability.

This F/A-18A, one of the VFA-136 Nighthawks, assigned to the Carrier USS Dwight D. Eisenhower provided air cover during the evacuation of foreign nationals in Monrovia, Liberia in 1990. (US Navy Photo)

A pair of F/A-18As aboard the USS Constellation in 1988 prepare for take-off. The aircraft are attached to the ship's catapult system at the center fuselage nose gear. Also note the blast deflector located immediately aft of the nearest Hornet. (McDonnell Douglas Photo)

During Desert Storm, Lt. Mike Mongillo of VFA-81 flies his F/A-18C back to the USS Saratoga in 1991. During the conflict, Mongillo was one of two Hornet pilots that shot down an Iraqi MiG-21 while on an attack mission. (McDonnell Douglas Photo)

A little message to Saddam was probably written by a crewman on a Mk 83 thousand pound bomb. The Hornet is assigned to VMFA-451, the Warlords. This Hornet is piloted by Col. M. A. Rietsch. (McDonnell Douglas Photo)

In addition to Navy Hornets, the Marine Corps also operates F/A-18s off Navy carriers. This photo shows an F/A-18A of VMFA-314, the Black Knights, preparing for take-off. (McDonnell Douglas Photo)

This F/A-18D of VMFA(AW)-121(The Green Knights) flies over burning Kuwaiti oil set on fire by order of Saddam Hussein. (McDonnell Douglas)

Two F/A-18D's of VMFA(AW)-121 fly in tight formation mounting wingtip Sidewinder missiles during Desert Storm. (McDonnell Douglas Photo)

There were two Navy Hornets lost to hostile fire with several others damaged by shoulder-launched SAM missiles, but all were repaired and returned to combat. Officials indicated that the critical element in that survivability was probably because of the location of the engine exhaust, which is far to the rear of most of the critical aircraft systems. One Hornet was hit by an Iraqi infrared missile, but flew back to base some 35 minutes distance without any oil pressure. And finally, all Navy MiG kills were recorded by Hornets.

Compared to the F-14s and A-6Es, which were the other Navy aircraft in Desert Storm, the F-18's reliability was far superior with 1.8 mean flight hours between failure. The model also showed a vast superiority over the same aircraft in maintainability and safety.

The Hornets were made from six carriers as follows: CV-62(USS Independence)—F/A-18Cs, CVN-69(USS Dwight D. Eisenhower)—F/A-18As, CV-60(USS Saratoga)—F/A-18Cs, CV-41(USS Midway)—F/A-18As, CV-66(USS

US Navy Lt Commander Mark Fox moves his F/A-18C into position for refueling as he returns from a mission during Desert Storm. Fox, from VFA-81 aboard the USS Saratoga, shot down an Iraqi MiG-21 on January 17, 1991 while he was on a bombing mission. This accomplishment points to the dual-role capabilities of the Hornet. (McDonnell Douglas Photo)

Five F/A-18Cs, from VFA-81, prepare for refueling from a USAF KC-135 tanker. Also note the A-6 Intruder, also awaiting fuel. The fact that this operation was carried out in daylight with so many aircraft demonstrates the complete air superiority that was quickly acquired in Desert Storm. (McDonnell Douglas Photo)

With Kuwait City in the background, this Green Knight F/A-18D banks to the left over the gulf. (McDonnell Douglas Photo)

Six Hornets from VMFA-314 fly over a Saudi Arabian facility. Note the Hornets on the ground sharing space with A-6s. This photo was taken during Desert Storm. (McDonnell Douglas Photo)

America(USS America)—F/A-18Cs and CVN-71(USS Theodore Roosevelt)—F/A-18As.

The planes came from the following units, respectively: VFA-25, VFA-113, VFA-131, VFA-136, VFA-81, VFA-83, VFA-192, VFA-195, VFA-82, VFA-86, VFA-15, and VFA-87.

Besides the obvious offensive missions that the Hornets accomplished during Desert Storm, there was also an important surveillance mission required of the model due to the absence of the SR-71 Blackbird. There were times when Hornets were sent up to survey the battlefield before they went on their operational missions. Commanders explained after the conflict that the F/A-18 fleet was able to place at least half of its bombs within 30 feet of the aim point. When compared with the accuracy demonstrated during World War II, this accomplishment is a hundred times more accurate.

A Navy official said the Hornets were the only aircraft in the conflict that successfully carried out both air superiority and air-to-ground operations on a single mission.

Marine F/A-18 aircraft were equally effective during the conflict with the main area of concentration being the 720

Three F/A-18Cs, part of VFA-81 Sunliners, return from a mission during Operation Desert Storm. Operating from the USS Saratoga in the Red Sea, Hornets from this squadron shot down two MiG-21s while on a bombing mission in Iraq. (McDonnell Douglas Photo)

An air-to-air right side view of a VFA-136 F/A-18C is flying over the nuclear powered USS Dwight D. Eisenhower as the vessel is underway in the Persian Gulf following Desert Storm. (US Navy Photo)

Post Desert Storm activities included Hornet deployments with the USS Abraham Lincoln in the Gulf of Oman. Here, a pair of F/A-18Cs from VFA-94(The Shrikes) are silhouetted against the sky during a late afternoon flight. The USS Lincoln operated in the Persian Gulf region during its first Western Pacific deployment. (DOD Photo)

artillery sites that threatened the route that the ground forces took in their advance. There was also a concerted effort against enemy vehicles and tanks.

Near the end of the war, one four-Hornet section enjoyed an amazing success when a major kill was accomplished including 19 tanks, nine armored personnel carriers, four rocket launchers,eight other vehicles, and a 60mm AA gun were all destroyed in a single day.

The Marines also had a dozen night-fighting F/A-18D aircraft which worked in concert with A-6s and EA-6B jamming aircraft. The Marine aircraft were all a part of the Marine Air Wing 3 (3rd MAW).

KUWAIT(POST DESERT STORM)
The post Desert Storm activity has seen F/A-18s in action again with those of the Kuwaiti Air Force's 40 Hornets being

An F/A-18A, from VMFA-531(The Gray Ghosts) monitors the flight of a Soviet Backfire bomber in June 1991. If this had been taken during the Cold War, the situation might have been more tense since the Russians were sympathetic to the US cause during Desert Storm. (McDonnell Douglas Photo)

An F/A-18C from VFA-147(The Argonauts) passes still-smoldering oil fields near Kuwait City during Operation Southern Watch, a multi-national effort establishing a no-fly zone for Iraqi aircraft south of the 32nd parallel in Iraq. The aircraft was assigned to the USS Nimitz. (DOD Photo)

Two Marine Corps F/A-18Ds from VMFA(AW)-533, The Hawks, carry laser-guided bombs on a training mission at Naval Air Station Fallon, NV. The Hawks, based at Marine Corp Air Station Beaufort, SC, have done two tours of duty at Aviano Air Base, Italy in support of UN and NATO operations in Bosnia-Herzegovina. In their second tour in 1995, the organization participated in the rescue of USAF Caption Scott O'Grady in June and were in the first wave of NATO air strikes against Bosnian Serb positions on August 30th. (McDonnell Douglas Photo)

a strong force in the area. The force flexed its muscle bigtime in October 1994 by flying bombing missions within sight of an Iraqi force deployed less than four miles from its borders. The Hornets are C and D models. The Hornets replaced the country's aging A-4 fleet.

The armament of the Kuwaiti planes consists of the MK 82 500 pound bombs, Mark 20 Rockeyes, along with AIM-9 and AIM-7 air-to-air missiles.

BOSNIA

The F/A-18 also played heavily in the Bosnia conflict commencing in 1993. In November of 1994, F/A-18Ds were part of the 30 plane group (also consisting of F-16Cs and F-15Es) which attacked Serb positions. Specific targets included artillery and theUbdina Airfield. During the mission, the Navy Hornets were subjected to surface-to-air missile attacks, but all returned safely to base. A month earlier, four Marine F-18Ds dropped thousand pound Mark 83 bombs and GBU-16 laser-guided bombs.

Navy F-18s also performed the air defense mission carrying the AGM-88 HARM missile. In August of 1995, the attacks took place again with more attacks on Serbian positions. More than 60 aircraft from NATO nations attacked positions around Sarajevo with the planes coming from Britain, Spain, France and the Dutch Air Force. Navy and Marine Hornets from the USS Theodore Roosevelt and the USS America as well as Marines from Aviano Air base were part of the US force.

With the signing of the peace accord in December of 1995, it would dictate Hornet involvement again in the region. Marine F/A-18Ds were outlined as strike aircraft. If radar-guided surface-to-air missiles became active, Marine and Navy EA-6Bs would produce refined target coordinates for both the F/A-18Ds and Air Force F-16s with the HARM Targeting System, which can carry anti-radiation missiles for attacking radars.

The Hornet's sensors can provide awareness to ensure that the HARM missiles are not fired at other than the desig-

A group of Marine F/A-18s were a part of a Combined Armed Exercise at Twenty-nine Palms in California's Mojave Desert. These Hornets are experiencing high-temperature conditions similar to those faced in Desert Storm. (McDonnell Douglas Photo)

nated targets. There are also the sensitive political boundaries to consider in this application.

The D Hornets also performed Forward Air Controller (FAC) functions where the pilot operated the aircraft while the back seater was responsible for monitoring action on the ground. The Hornet crewmen had at their disposal two FLIR sensors and night vision goggles to identify both hostile and friendly forces on the ground.

It was also pointed out that the D Hornets would also be used in an air control function supporting ground forces. Officials explained that the Hornet was the only aircraft with that capability.

CHINA

In early 1996, the Hornet again was brought in harm's way when China was firing missiles into the sea near Taiwan. Hornets were aboard the USS Independence which was cruising in the general area. Fortunately, the Hornets were not called into action.

OTHER HORNET IMPLICATIONS

There is in the mid-1990s discussions at high levels as to what role the Marines should play in future battlefields with its own tactical air support. Part of that capability is about the Corp's 192 F/A-18s and 20 EA-6B Prowler electronic warfare aircraft. It has been discussed that the Air Force or Navy could fulfill this role. The Marines argue that with its own air defense capability, it can deploy more quickly and more effectively.

The Marines demonstrated their arguments with a three-week exercise in 1994 dubbed CAX-4-94 held in the Mojave Desert in California. The operation used 20 Hornets from Marine Corps Air Station Beaufort, South Carolina and six AV-8B Harriers from Marine Corps Air Station Cherry Point, North Carolina. Marine officials indicated that the exercise provided a realistic combat environment with the opportunity to drop live ordnance and show ground commanders what their aircraft can do.

Furthering that situation in late 1995 was the assertion by the Air Force that the Marine buy of Super Hornets should be eliminated giving the close ground support mission responsibility completely to the Air Force. Needless to say, that proposition certainly didn't meet with much of a positive view from the Marines. The Air Force argued that the tactical aircraft of the three services had overlapping roles.

The down-sloping wings in the foreground belong to Marine Corp AV-8B Harriers face a hive of Hornets. These aircraft were on the flight line at an expeditionary airfield at Marine Corp Armed Exercise at Twenty-nine Palms, California in 1994.

Chapter 6:
The F-18E/F-The Ultimate Hornet

The story of how the F-18E/F came to be is very interesting to say the least. When you think about it, it could really be called the third choice of the future fighter deliberations that occurred in the 1980s.

But the success of the earlier Hornet versions certainly helped the E/F version come to be. Later in the program, the third version of the Hornet would somewhat shed its E/F designation, being called the more appropriate 'Super Hornet' nomenclature. With the improvement of performance across the board for the new plane, 'Super' was a definite descriptor.

The story of the third model Hornet actually begins with the canceled A-12, a highly-classified machine that was to be the answer for all the Navy's problems. The implications of the cancellation were significant in that it was meant to replace the aging USAF F-111 fleet and other models.

The program had fallen badly behind schedule. The money invested was getting completely out of hand and Secretary of Defense Cheney canceled the program. A fleet of 620 A-12s had been planned at a cost of about $80 million each.

Interestingly, there had been two other proposals for the A-12 competition, both extensive modifications to existing Navy fighters. First, there was the Tomcat-21, a greatly upgraded version of the proven Navy F-14 Tomcat. Then, there was the McDonnell Douglas Hornet 2000, which would eventually evolve into the F/A-18E/F. It was reported that the F/A-18 variant came in third in the competition.

One of the first looks at the E/F version is provided by this 1993 company artist concept. Marked differences between the earlier versions include rectangular intakes, lack of an air brake, and increased size. (McDonnell Douglas Photo)

This 1994 artist concept depicts an E/F air-to-air mission against a MiG-29. The new Hornet was advertised as having greater endurance, more payload carrying ability and increased carrier bring-back capability. (McDonnell Douglas Photo)

The E/F can refuel other fighters in flight. The Strike Fighter, in this 1993 artist concept, is shown with an aerial refueling store on the centerline and two 480 gallon external fuel tanks. Also depicted on outboard pylons are AIM-9 Sidewinders and on fuselage engine intake are AIM-120 AMRAAM missiles. The AGM-84E SLAM missiles are located on mid-wing pylons. (McDonnell Douglas Photo)

In 1991, the AX program was born, a plane to supposedly replace the canceled A-12, a plane which would fulfill a long range, all-weather strike mission. It was basically what had been planned for the A-12, but the approach was to be different.

Stealth characteristics were planned for the plane along with the capability to carry advanced air launched missiles.

Planning called for 234 AX aircraft to be in front line service by 2010.

With that kind of leadtime before operational service was in place for the AX, it was decided that there would have to be something to fill the gap. Reenter the advanced F-18 version again, with the FY92-93 budget calling for $1.4 billion for the work to commence on the so-called F-18E/F. Planning at

In September 1995, the first F/A-18E was dedicated at the McDonnell Douglas plant in St. Louis.

This rear view of the initial E version shows the large trailing edge flaps, the characteristic four control surface tail, and larger body strake. (McDonnell Douglas Photo)

ABOVE/OPPOSITE TOP: The size comparison between the old and the new is vividly illustrated here. The E version is in the foreground which has two additional weapon stations, 34 inches longer, and the wings are 25 percent larger than those of the C version in the back-ground. As can be seen, the 20mm Gatling Gun was retained in the new Hornet in the same nose position. (McDonnell Douglas Photo)

Final assembly of one of the first Super Hornet is shown in the final process at the McDonnell Douglas St. Louis facility. (McDonnell Douglas Photo)

the time called for the modified Hornet to start replacing the early F/A-18As in the late 1990s.

Among the industry teams bidding for the AX program, there were: (1) a team of Lockheed, Boeing, and General Dynamics proposing a version of the Air Force F-22, (2) a team of Lockheed, Boeing, and Grumman offering a new design, (3) a team of McDonnell-Douglas and General Dynamics offering an improved A-12, (4) a joint McDonnell/LTV proposal, and (5) a new design from Northrop. Projected as one of the biggest programs left in the century, it's easy to understand the great interest.

Then, like the earlier A-12, the AX would also see the ax fall on it too, making the F-18E/F the only program still in existence. What had previously been thought of as only a gap-filler was now the only active program. So here's the story of the E/F and how it evolved.

The E/F story actually began in the mid-1980s, when early F/A-18 versions demonstrated versatility, reliability, maintainability, and affordability over its entire life cycle prompted interest in an evolutionary upgrade to fulfill the Navy's strike

No mistaking the shape of the F-A-18E/F forward fuselage as it is prepared to join the rear portion of the fuselage. (McDonnell Douglas Photo)

fighter requirement into the next century, actually 20 years into the next century.

The F/A-18 E/F grew out of a 1987 study requested by then Secretary of Defense Caspar Weinberger. The study was conducted by the Naval Air Systems Command(NAVAIR), McDonnell Douglas and Northrop Grumman, and defined several potential approaches for the new Hornet. The resulting E/F was the final configuration decided upon by the Navy.

Quite simply, the F/A-18 E/F from its nomenclature appears to be the next modification of the Hornet following the A-D models. But the latest version is MUCH more than that, practically being a new aircraft. The E/F could well have been given a completely-new number designation because of its extensive redesign, but that didn't happen.

The fitting of the first E/F bulkhead is shown in process in this 1994 photo. It would be the first of many, many to follow. (McDonnell Douglas Photo)

The first E version takes off from St. Louis's Lambert International Airport with McDonnell Douglas pilot Fred Madenwald at the controls. Take-off was 11:55AM CST on November 29, 1995. The Navy planned at the time to purchase one thousand E/Fs through 2015. The aircraft was scheduled to go into operational service in 2001. (McDonnell Douglas Photo)

The first F version is shown in its second test flight on May 20, 1996 near St. Louis. The first flight was April 1, 1996. The F1 aircraft was ferried to Naval Air Station Patuxent River Maryland in May 1996. The aircraft was planned for sea trials in 1997. (McDonnell Douglas Photo)

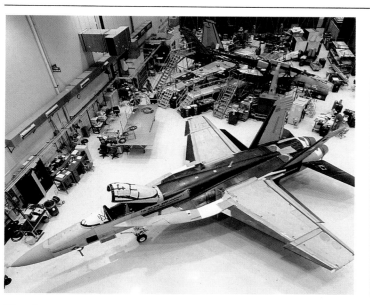

The first two E models, E1 and E2, are shown in final assembly in August 1995 at the St. Louis McDonnell Douglas facility. (McDonnell Douglas Photo)

The situation was similar to that of the USAF F-15E, a major redesign of the basic F-15 design which still carried the F-15 Eagle designation.

The enhancements for the E/F offered longer range, greater endurance, higher payload capability, more powerful engines, increased carrier bringback capability, enhanced survivability and a renewed potential for future growth.

As was the case with the earlier A through D versions, the E/F version would be tested heavily (in subscale form) at the Arnold Engineering Development Center(AEDC), Tennessee. The E/F underwent store separation tests that helped predict how missiles and fuel tanks would separate from the plane when released in flight and verification of the inlet configuration for the design through various speed ranges and angles of attack. The testing was accomplished in Arnold's 16-foot tunnel.

Finally, in 1993, Arnold accomplished hundreds of hours of testing on the E/F's F414 powerplant which covered its complete altitude envelope. During the testing, AEDC engineers used a laser measurement system to precisely measure nozzle position, and gas sampling technology to help characterize conditions in the engine's afterburner section.

During 1996, new materials used in the wing skin panels and fuel cells successfully passed live-fire testing. The tests were conducted at the Navy Weapons Survivability Laboratory at China Lake, California. The testing indicated that the new polyurethane fuel cells would be able to withstand the impact of armor-piercing ammunition.

NASA was also involved with the E/F test program in the mid-1990s. The program called for some 50 flights using a free-flight model to (1) determine the plane's low-speed en-

The second E test aircraft, designated E2, makes its fifth functional test flight on February 17, 1996 near McDonnell Douglas, St. Louis. It first flew on December 26, 1995. It is now part of a three year flight test program at Naval Air Station Patuxent River Maryland. (McDonnell Douglas Photo)

The fourth F/A-18E test model is in the final assembly area at the McDonnell Douglas manufacturing facility in St. Louis. This aircraft entered the flight test program in September, 1996. (McDonnell Douglas Photo)

The distinctive features of the F/A-E/F are visible in this underside view. This Hornet has rectangular engine inlets unlike the rounded intakes of the A-D versions and bears a marked similarity to those of the USAF F-15. Also, this model sports a larger, more curved leading edge extension. (McDonnell Douglas Photo)

velope and (2) to predict the vehicle's behavior during highly dynamic conditions. The data would be used in the E/F's flight test program which would be conducted concurrently.

The 400-pound model was a 22 percent scale representation of the real item with the majority of the drops being made from about 12,000 feet with about a minute and one-half flight time. The extensive testing was deemed necessary because of the significant changes made to this third version of the Hornet.

It was felt the modified leading edge extensions might alter the spin recovery characteristics and vortex flows, which would be considerably different than the F/A-18's initial design.

The design goals for the plane were extremely high in just about every aspect of the plane:

Reliability:1.8 mean flight hours between failure ascompared with 0.5 hours for the F-14 andA-6E,

Maintainability:57.8 flight hours per maintenance flight hours as compared to 21.5(F-14) and 22.5 for the A-6E,

Safety: 21,300 flight hours between losses as compared to 12,300(A-6E) and 14,800 for the F-14.

But it wasn't all 'wine and roses' for the E/F during its early development days as the plane was well overweight during its early design phase. And with the way that so many programs in the past had been canceled, the Navy was definitely worried about its new fighter. Then, there was also a threat to the program when the possibility of the Navy being forced to accept the F-14D upgrade. Had that happened, it is unlikely that the E/F would have ever evolved, with additional buys of the C/D version probably being substituted.

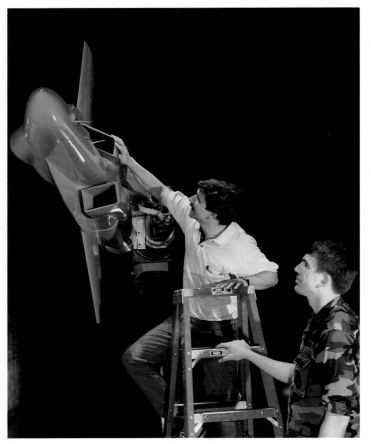

1993 tests to support the development of the E/F were conducted in the Air Force's Arnold Engineering Development Center's(AEDC) 16 foot supersonic wind tunnel. Consolidation of work has led DOD test centers to perform work for the other services. (USAF Photo)

A scale E/F model at AEDC's 16 foot wind tunnel underwent inlet validation tests to assure proper air flow to the fighter's jet engines. (USAF Photo)

This 1995 wind tunnel test of the E/F was to certify that a munition will separate safely and effectively in flight. Such tests are frequently carried out with models upside-down in the tunnel. (USAF Photo)

Volume changes to the advanced F/A-18 increased the internal fuel capacity by 3,600 pounds, the equivalent of about 33 percent. The increase extends the Hornet's range by some 40 percent. In the avionics area, though, the E/F retains about 90 percent commonality with the earlier C/D versions.

Structural changes with the E/F are significant with the fuselage stretched by 34 inches, along with an enlarged wing area of an additional 100 square feet-the equivalent of a 25 percent larger wing over the 400 square feet of the earlier Hornet configurations.

The larger wing improves flight characteristics and included additional external weapons stations designed to carry a variety of technologically-advanced air-to-air and air-to-ground weapons. The advanced F414 powerplant, will increase the Hornet's total thrust from 36,000 (Late model C/Ds) to 44,000 pounds. The increased thrust improves the E/F's subsonic, transonic, and supersonic performance, leading to better overall performance. Much of the increased thrust capabilities of the F414 is acquired from enlarged air inlets providing increased airflow into the engine.

Each of the 22,000 pound thrust powerplants weighs about 2,445 pounds, which equates to an impressive thrust-to-weight ratio for each engine of about 9-1. The core of the engine is based on the GE 412, which had been previously selected to power the canceled A-12. Also incorporated in this advanced powerplant is an afterburner, a 35-inch-diameter fan, and a low-pressure turbine section.

Interestingly, the Navy didn't see fit to conduct a competition for the E/F powerplant, instead awarding the contract on a sole-source basis to General Electric. At the time of con-

tract awarding in 1991, GE was given $500M for development in what was estimated at the time as a possible $4 billion engine contract over the duration of the program.

True, the powerplants for the E/F are more powerful, but this is a considerably larger aircraft than its older brothers.

The E/F, for example, has a maximum take-off weight of just over 66,000 pounds compared to only 51,900 pounds for the F/A-18C version.

Much of the extra weight comes from the increased fuel load the E/F can carry. For example, internal fuel capacity was increased to 14,500 pounds(up from 10,900 pounds). The new Hornet also has the capability to carry external 480 gallon tanks(capable of carrying 9,800 pounds of jet fuel) as compared to only 330-gallon tanks on the C/D.

Advanced materials play heavily in the construction of the E/F with extensive use of carbon/epoxy material. Use of the material is found in the leading edge flap along with the center and aft fuselage.

The crew station and survivability aspects of the new plane have also been enhanced. Changes in the crew station include a touch-sensitive up-front control display and the six-inch-square Tactical Situation Display, which replaces the current five-by-five inch display, which allows pilots to take full advantage of the C/D's multi-source integration (MSI) software. Interestingly, in the two-seat F model, both the front and rear crew stations are identical.

The E/F upgrade provides growth capability to incorporate future avionics and other weapon system improvements that may be needed to counter changes in adversary capabilities. Growth provisions such as liquid and air cooling, in-

"Loaded to the hilt" would have to be the description of this weapons loading test on the E/F. Note the instrumentation the weapons on the three pylons under each wing. (McDonnell Douglas Photo)

McDonnell Douglas is shown testing the E/F's General Electric F414-GE-400 engines in 1995. Due to their size, these 22,000 pound thrust engines cannot be retrofitted to earlier Hornet versions. These engines produce 35 percent more thrust than the A-D version powerplants. (McDonnell Douglas Photo)

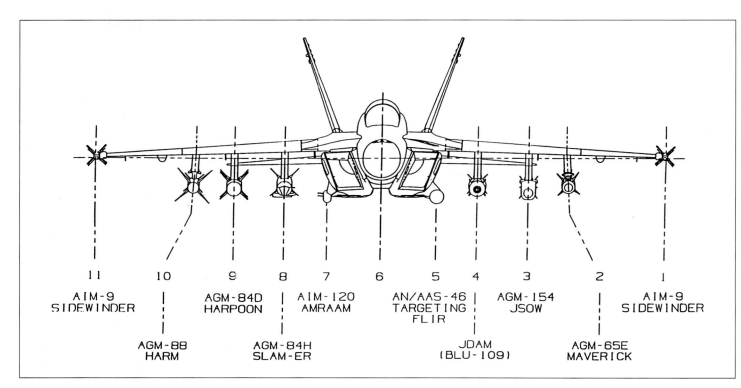

This company line drawing shows the weapons suite for the E/F. Note the variety of both air-to-air and air-to-surface weapons that can be carried. (McDonnell Douglas Drawing)

This view of an F/A-18E/F cockpit simulator shows the pilot's eye view of the displays including three new active matrix liquid crystal displays. At top center, the touch screen up-front control display replaces the A-D's mechanical up-front control panel. At bottom(center), a 6.25x6.25 inch multi-purpose color display replaces the A-D 5x5 inch cathode ray tube display. And, at bottom left, an easier to comprehend engine/fuel display replaces the A-D digital watch type liquid crystal readout. Kaiser Electronics, San Jose, CA, designed the elaborate displays. (McDonnell Douglas photo)

creased electrical capacity, and more internal space for avionics "black boxes" are included so that, if a new threat arises, the advanced Hornet will permit the Navy and Marine Corps to rapidly integrate an appropriate countermeasure.

The E/F uses much of the existing hardware and components of earlier Hornets. For example, considerable C/D avionics systems and software are a part of the E/F.

The E/F also built upon several incremental upgrades to systems that had been completed, or that were underway, on the C/D version. The most significant among these was an upgrade to the already-effective APG-65 radar, which will increase the speed and memory of the radar's signal and data processors.

Due to the increased effectiveness of the APG-65 modification, it was decided to rename the system the APG-73. That advanced system, by the way, was included as a part of C/D deliveries after June 1994.

As the E/F neared initial production, refinements continued on the new fighter. For example, McDonnell Douglas significantly reduced the radar visibility (radar cross section) on all the antennae carried by the version.

Just looking at the E/F design, it's easy to note that the design is far from a pure stealthy configuration. But measures were taken to reduce the radar image that might appear on enemy radar screens. One of the main areas addressed was a re-design of the engine inlets. The plane isalso equipped with a doubling of the number of chaff-and-flare expendables.

Under development in the 1990s for the E/F (and possibly for the USAF's B-1B, F-15E, U-2, and F-22) is the "smart" towed decoy—part of the Navy's Integrated Defensive Electronic Countermeasures system. This decoy radiates appropriate microwave frequencies to invite attacks from enemy missiles.

Stealth considerations for the new plane were manifested with the use of radar-absorbing material (RAM) on the plane. One location where RAM material was extensively used was the engine inlets where a 'bump' was added inside the engine inlets to partially block the faces of the engines. McDonnell Douglas engineers indicated that additional modifications can be made to the model to meet any future threats.

Since weapon delivery is an important part of the mission of any attack aircraft, ordnance-carrying capability was

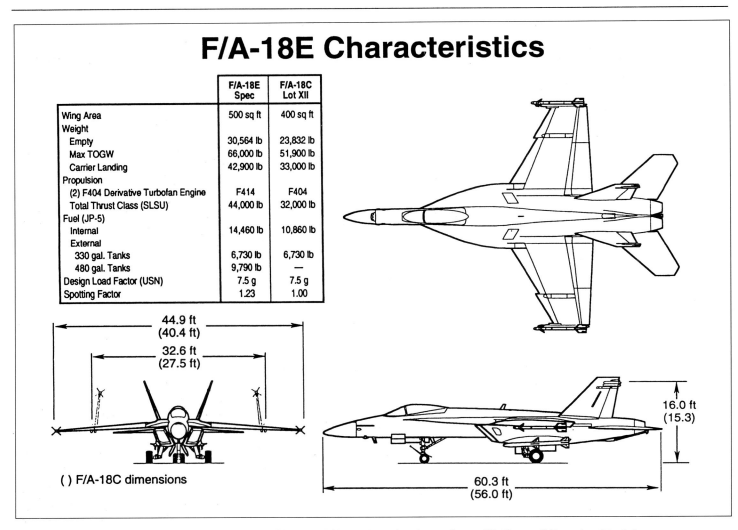

F/A-18E Characteristics

	F/A-18E Spec	F/A-18C Lot XII
Wing Area	500 sq ft	400 sq ft
Weight		
Empty	30,564 lb	23,832 lb
Max TOGW	66,000 lb	51,900 lb
Carrier Landing	42,900 lb	33,000 lb
Propulsion		
(2) F404 Derivative Turbofan Engine	F414	F404
Total Thrust Class (SLSU)	44,000 lb	32,000 lb
Fuel (JP-5)		
Internal	14,460 lb	10,860 lb
External		
330 gal. Tanks	6,730 lb	6,730 lb
480 gal. Tanks	9,790 lb	—
Design Load Factor (USN)	7.5 g	7.5 g
Spotting Factor	1.23	1.00

44.9 ft
(40.4 ft)

32.6 ft
(27.5 ft)

16.0 ft
(15.3)

60.3 ft
(56.0 ft)

( ) F/A-18C dimensions

A comparison of the facts and figures for the C/D and E/F versions is shown here. (McDonnell Douglas Photo)

a big consideration in the design of the E/F. To that end, two additional weapon stations were added to the plane.

For different mission scenarios, there are different weapon loadings for the E/F. For the Combat Air Patrol Endurance mission, the new Hornet carries two AIM-9 and four AIM-120 missiles.

For the Fighter Escort role, it's two AIM-9 and two AIM-120 missiles, while the Interdiction Mission shows two AIM-9s, four MK-83 bombs, and two external fuel tanks.

As the E/F was to be the only active Navy program for many years to come, the Navy has considered a number of different missions for the model in addition to the prime air defense and ground attack missions.

First considered was an electronic jamming version called the F/A-18 Command and Control Warfare (C2W) variant as a potential successor to the Navy's EA-6B. Test results in the mid-1990s were so encouraging that they prompted McDonnell Douglas to take a look at outfitting USAF F-15Es with the same C2W equipment.

Also, in 1993, due to the retirement of existing KA-6D and S-3 tankers, there was consideration for possible conversion of some of the advanced Hornets into tankers.

In 1996, the F/A-18 was also considered as a potential future replacement for the aging EA-6B jammer aircraft. It seems that the types of potential missions of this magnificent bird are unlimited.

The first Super Hornet(a single-seat F-18E which was so monogrammed on the upper fuselage) took off from St Louis Lambert International Airport on November 29, 1995, marking the beginning of the extensive flight test program. That first Super Hornet was designated the E-1. The program consisted of seven R&D aircraft to prove the flight characteristics of the new strike fighter.

The second E flight test version was designated E-2, while the first F version was the F-1 aircraft. That test plane was used primarily for testing the plane's suitability for carrier operations. As of August 1996, the F-1 had made three catapult 11 launches from a land-based system which simulated car-

The F/A-18E/F and C/D Comparison

	F/A-18E/F	F/A-18C/D
Type	Single-seat (E) and two-seat (F) twin-turbofan tactical aircraft	Single-seat (C) and two-seat (D) twin-turbofan tactical aircraft
First Flight	December 1995	November 1978 (F/A-18A/B)
Propulsion	Two GE F414 turbofan engines, producing 44,000 pounds of combined thrust (22,000 pounds each)	Enhanced Performance (EPE): Two GE F404-GE-402 engines, producing 35,400 pounds of combined thrust (17,700 pounds each)
Radar	Hughes APG-73 multimedia radar	Hughes APG-73 multimedia radar
Length	60.3 feet	56 feet
Height	16 feet	15.3 feet
Wingspan	44.9 feet (with wing-tip missiles)	40.4 feet (with wing-tip missiles)
Speed	Mach 1.8-plus	Mach 1.8 plus
Combat Ceiling	50,000 feet	50,000 feet
Combat Radius	660-plus nm (1188-plus km)	470-plus nm (846-plus km)
Empty Weight	30,500 pounds (approx.)	23,800 pounds (approx.)
MTOGW	66,000 pounds (approx.)	51,900 pounds (approx.)
Fuel	14,508 pounds internal 9,800 pounds in three 480-gallon external tanks or 6,700 pounds in three 330-gallon external tanks	10,381 pounds internal 6,700 pounds in three 330-gallon external tanks
Internal Armament	Lightweight M61A1 20mm cannon with 400 rounds of ammunition	Lightweight M61A1 20mm cannon with 578 rounds of ammunition
Weapons Stations	11 wing and fuselage stations	9 wing and fuselage stations
External Payload	Up to 17,750 pounds maximum	Up to 14,900 punds maximum

Both payloads include wearons, sensors, and fuel tanks. Weapons includ AIM-9 Sidewinder, AIM-7 Sparrow, AIM-120 AMRAAM Harpoon, HARM, Shrike, SLAM, SLAM-ER, Walleye and Maverick TV-, laser- and infrared-guided missiles. Joint Stand-Off Weapon (JSOW); Joint Direct Attack Munition (JDAM); various current and planned general purpose bombs, mines, and rockets.

rier deck operations. The test took place at Patuxent River.

The E-4 test plane was used primarily for high angle of attack applications. The first flight of E-5 was planned for September 1996, a test plane dedicated to weapon development and integration. The F-2 version was also planned for evaluation of weapons separation.

Plans in late 1995 also called for the modification of an existing C/D version for the testing of the new avionics. In addition to the flying testbeds, there were also three ground-based versions-static test, drop test, and fatigue test-that would be utilized for design verification at the McDonnell St. Louis facility.

During 1996, it was announced that the ECC International Corp of Wayne, PA was awarded a $23.2 million contract to provide simulators for training E/F maintenance personnel.

As the production phase of the plane neared, there was considerable engine testing accomplished by General Electric on the craft's F414 derivative engines.

Like any recent high-cost, high-tech weapons system, the F/A-18 was forced to endure heavy scrutinizing from many quarters with other large programs as the B-2 Bomber, and V-22 tiltrotor transport all clamoring for funds. Whether the Navy will get its desired thousand E/F versions remains to be seen. Production, though, was approved in the 1996 budget for an even dozen E/Fs, a small but significant step.

As is the case with any high-dollar weapon system in the downsizing military in the 1990s, the E/F has had its share of criticism. The General Accounting Office(GAO) was one of the most critical when it reported that the Pentagon could save "almost $17 billion if it would abandon the thousand plane E/F program and instead buy additional C/D versions. The report added that the operational deficiencies used to justify the E/F had not materialized or could be corrected with upgrades to the C/D."

Needless to say, the Navy didn't agree with those findings and hopes that the E/F will survive in the numbers it desires.

Only time will tell, of course.

Chapter 7:
Foreign Hornets

Foreign F/A-18s are landbased fighters and to date eight nations outside the U.S. either have or will have Hornets in their inventories. As of late 1996, those countries flying A/Bs include: Canada—138, Australia—75, and Spain—72; those flying C/Ds include Kuwait—40, Finland—7 delivered of 64 ordered, Switzerland—1 delivered of 34 ordered, Malaysia—8 ordered, and Thailand—8 ordered.

Canada

Canada, in the late 1970s, wanted a single type of fighter to replace its aging F-101 Voodoos and F-104 Starfighters. It needed an aircraft which could operate reliably and routinely over large, open and sparsely populated areas common in Canada. And because of its North Atlantic Treaty Organization commitments, it also needed a fighter which could handle trans-Atlantic ferry missions. For these reasons and the opinion that the F/A-18 offered the potential for greater growth than did its competitor, the F-16, Canadian Armed Forces officials chose the F/A-18.

Canada became the first export customer for the F/A-18 and received the first of these fighters in October 1982 for 410 Operational Training Squadron, Cold Lake, Alberta. Designated CF-18s, the Canadian version doesn't carry the Hornet nickname because the word in French doesn't have the same meaning.

The CF-18 carries a special cold weather land survival pack and an instrument landing system and some of its pilots are women. Other Canada-specific features include provisions for LAU 5003 rocket pods which can contain 19 Bristol Aerospace CRV-7 2.75 rockets and BL755 cluster bombs and a 600,000 candlepower searchlight in the starboard nose for night interceptions. The CF-18 now is operational in seven squadrons; three in the intercept and four in the attack roles. Deliveries were completed in 1988. Canada flies 98 CF-18As and 40 CF-18Bs.

The Canadian CF-18s, because of large open and sparsely populated areas, are equipped with special cold weather land survival packs. Women pilots routinely fly Canadian CF-18s in operations. (McDonnell Douglas Photo)

This Canadian CF-18A is shown in joint exercises with a Soviet MiG fighter. All Canadian F-18s are A/B versions, a total of 138 being purchased. (McDonnell Douglas Photo)

This Canadian Hornet carries two 480 gallon external fuel tanks, the same capacity tanks which will be carried by the USN E/F versions. Canada required the larger than the standard US A-D 330 gallon tanks because of the large distances over wilderness areas. (McDonnell Douglas Photo)

Australia

Australia took a six-year look at fighter candidates to replace its 21-year-old fleet of Dassault Mirages. The Royal Australian Air Force (RAAF), realizing that Australia's operating environments were similar to those of Canada, recommended buying the F/A-18. Some deciding factors were: twin-engine safety, low attrition rate, advanced avionics, ease of maintenance, performance and growth potential (RAAF expectations were justified based upon the 1985 performance of the F/A-18 during a U.S. Marine exercise in Egypt which demonstrated the aircraft's operability in extreme temperatures and minimal backup—conditions similar to what it might face in Australia).

The Operational Conversion Unit, RAAF Base Williamtown began receiving F/A-18s in May 1985. They're also based at RAAF Base Tindal. RAAF Hornets are assembled in Australia as are its F404 engines. Scheduled de-

The familiar kangaroo insignia indicates that this F/A-18A is in the Royal Australian Air Force. The country started receiving its 75 A/B Hornets(land-based only) in 1985. (McDonnell Douglas Photo)

Spain began delivery of its A/B Hornets in 1986, the first European customer. The country has 60 A versions and 12 B versions(shown here) and are locally designated C.15 and CE.15, respectively.

liveries were completed in 1990 but there is some interest in a future reconnaissance version.

The RAAF Hornet has no catapult launch equipment but has a conventional instrument landing system and an added high frequency radio for long-range communications. Australia flies 57 F/A-18As and 18 F/A-18Bs.

Spain

The Spanish Air Force Hornets, called EF-18s, began delivery in early 1986 and Spain became the first F/A-18 customer in Europe. Its 60 EF-18As and 12 EF-18B two seat trainers have the local designations C.15 and CE.15 respectively (the "E" stands for Espana).

With an initial arrangement with the U.S. Navy, Spain's firm, CASA, became responsible for overhauls of Hornets—including those of the U.S. and Canada—in the Mediterranean. It is capable of maintaining 95 percent of avionics, 80 percent of the airframe and 100 percent of the F404. The SAF flies its EF-18s from air bases at Zaragoza and Torrejon. Spain is negotiating a buy of 24 early-model F/A-18s from the U.S. Navy inventory and plans to base them at Moron.

In the early to mid-1990s, Spanish Hornets underwent upgrades to F/A-18A+/B+ with new computers, software, wiring and pylon modifications approaching the C/D configuration.

Spanish Hornet equipment includes: wingtip AIM-9L sidewinder air-to-air missiles, underwing AIM-7 Sparrows and a variety of bombs. It also carries AGM-88 HARM anti-radiation missiles and AGM-84 Harpoon anti-ship missiles. For protection, Spanish F/A-18s are equipped with Sanders AN/ALQ-126B deception jammers; the last 36 aircraft ordered carry Northrop AN/ALQ-162(V) systems.

This Royal Kuwaiti Air Force F/A-18C was the first production Hornet powered by GE's F404-402 Enhanced Performance Engines which can produce from 10-20 percent more thrust than previous F404 engines. (McDonnell Douglas Photo)

Receiving a total of 64 C/D Hornets, Finland will assemble 57 of them in Finland. Here is the first D version being delivered from McDonnell Douglas. (McDonnell Douglas Photo)

Kuwait

To bolster its small air force and replace its Mirage F.1CK and A-4KU Skyhawk fighters, Kuwait selected the F/A-18. In September 1988, Kuwait ordered 32 F/A-18Cs and eight F/A-18Ds in a package along with AGM-65G Mavericks, AGM-84 Harpoons, AIM-7F Sparrows and AIM-9L Sidewinders. The first Kuwait Air Force F/A-18C/D flew in September 1991 and was the first production F/A-18 powered by GE's new F404-GE-402 Enhanced Performance Engines which can produce from 10 to 20 percent more thrust than previous F404 engines.

Deliveries of the first three two-seaters were accepted by No. 25 Squadron of the Kuwaiti Air Force in January 1992. Deliveries were completed in August 1993 and Kuwaiti Hornets are based at Al Jaber Air Base, new Kuwait City. There is speculation by some sources that the country will order more Hornets and Kuwait indicated that it wishes to buy AIM-120 Advanced Medium Range Air-to-Air Missiles.

Finland

After an intensive aircraft evaluation process involving the F/A-18, F-16, Mirage 2000-5 and JAS-39 Gripen, Finland selected the Hornet in May 1992. The 64 Finnish F/A-18s will replace the MiG-21 air defense fighters now in use. The Finnish Air Force received seven complete D models: four in November 1995 and three in early 1996.

The buy specifies final assembly and ramp operations of the remaining 57 Hornets performed by Valmet Aviation Inc., Halli, Finland. The first Valmet-assembled F/A-18C flew May 14, 1996. The company delivered this aircraft to the Finnish Air Force in 1996. Finnish Hornets will feature the Dash 402 enhanced performance engines, upgraded Hughes APG-73 radar systems, and modern air-to-air missiles.

This Royal Kuwaiti Air Force F/A-18D was one of eight D versions ordered by this Middle East country. There were also 32 C versions ordered. These 40 planes were part of a package with a number of air-to-air and air-to-surface missiles. (McDonnell Douglas Photo)

One of the reasons that Finland selected the Hornet was its cold weather capabilities. Shown here is a F/A-18D during Finnish Air Force flight evaluation in February 1992. (McDonnell Douglas Photo)

The Swiss Air Force received the first of its 34 F/A-18 Hornets in January 1996. Most of them will be assembled in Switzerland, the first expected to fly in late 1996 and delivered to the Swiss Air Force in early 1997. (McDonnell Douglas Photo)

Although appearing completely different from normal Hornets, these in fact belong to the US Navy as a part of the Adversary Squadron in Fallon, Nevada. They are designed to represent foreign air-to-air threats. (McDonnell Douglas Photo)

The first Malaysian F/A-18 will roll out in ceremonies at McDonnell Douglas in 1997. Malaysia ordered eight D versions to complement its small fleet of MiG-29s. (McDonnell Douglas Photo)

Security cooperation among Scandinavian nations is receiving high priority as they move toward closer ties both economic and political with the rest of Europe. However, the impact of Finland's selection of the F/A-18 for air force modernization is difficult to determine as of this writing.

Switzerland
In the summer of 1991, Switzerland's Federal Military Department announced its recommendation to buy the F/A-18. Hornets will replace Hawker Hunter, F-5 International Fighter and Dassault Mirage III fighters and be used especially for the air defense role. The recommendation cited the F/A-18's overall performance during a two-month flight evaluation, its all-weather capability, reliable radar and avionics systems, low operational and support costs, and growth potential. Other contenders were the F-16, MiG-29, and Mirage 2000-5.

The maiden flight of Switzerland's first F/A-18D was January 20, 1996. This and a Swiss F/A-18C underwent weapons system testing for several months before planned delivery to Switzerland in December 1996 and early 1997 respectively. As of late 1996, the 32 remaining Swiss F/A-18s were undergoing final assembly and ramp operations at the Swiss Aircraft and Systems Co., Emmen, near Lucerne, Switzerland.

The first Hornet assembled in Switzerland is scheduled to fly in late 1996 and be delivered to the Swiss Air Force in early 1997. Swiss Hornets feature the enhanced performance version of the F404 engine.

Malaysia
The first F/A-18 for Malaysia is scheduled to roll out in a ceremony at McDonnell Douglas, St. Louis in 1997. Malaysia ordered the Hornet to complement its MiG-29s. The split buy will replace the very outdated F-5.

Thailand
Since it already operates 36 Lockheed Martin F-16s, the Thai government's decision to buy eight F/A-18s surprised many aerospace watchers in 1996. The multirole Hornets will carry out air-to-air, maritime and air-to-ground strike missions and complement the F-16 fleet. Other competitors included the Mirage 2000-5, SU-27, MiG-29, and F-16.

The Thai Hornets will be powered by GE's enhanced performance F404 engines and the fighter package will include AIM-120 Advanced Medium Range Air-to-Air Missiles. Thailand is expected to begin receiving four "C"s and four "D"s in 1999.

Chapter 8:
The F/A-18 and the Blue Angels

At the end of World War II, Admiral Chester Nimitz-then Chief of Naval Operations, ordered the formation of a flight demonstration team to keep the public interested in naval aviation.

The Blue Angels performed their first flight demonstration less than a year later in June 1946 at their home base, Naval Air Station(NAS), Jacksonville, Florida. The first plane selected was a World War star, the Grumman F6F Hellcat.

But the Hellcat's stay was short as only two months later, the team transitioned to the GrummanF8F Bearcat and introduced the famous diamond configuration. At the end of the decade, the team was flying its first jet aircraft, the Grumman F9F-2 Panther. Interestingly, the team would be called intact to combat duty to support the Korean War effort.

The following year, the team was reorganized with the newer and faster F9F-5 Panther. In 1954, it was then on to an ever-later Panther version, the F9F-8.

In 1974, the A-4F Skyhawk II became the next Blue Angel aircraft of choice. Always desiring the to utilize the latest fighter available, it wasn't surprising that a move was made to the F/A-18A, a change that occurred in November 1986. As of the middle of the 1990s, the Hornet still holds that vaunted position and should remain there for many years to come.

The Blue Angel F/A-18As carry the characteristic and longstanding blue and yellow color scheme with the blue being the predominant color. The yellow is used mostly to detail

the planes adorning the stabilizer tops and sweeping around behind and them forward of the cockpit. The Blue Angel crest sits on the forward fuselage with the Blue Angel name scripted just forward of the engine intake. The paint scheme seems to give the aircraft more of a sleek and menacing look.

Blue Angel officials indicated that the paint jobs on the aircraft hold up well. But with the large number of shows the team gives, there are nicks and scratches that periodically have to be touched up. However, the complete repaint of any of the Angel Hornets is a rare occurrence.

But it must be remembered that these Hornets are first and always combat aircraft, and they must be able to be quickly converted back to their combat configurations. Blue Angel officials indicated that the transition 'could be accomplished within hours.'

Of course, the demonstration F/A-18s carry no ordnance. Also, the nose cannon has been removed and its volume has been filled with a smoke generator. About the only other modification to the Angel configuration is the installation of special fuel pumps for the significant amount of up-side-down flight.

The particular Hornets that are used by the Blue Angels are some of the oldest in the inventory, coming from a lot of planes produced in the early 1980s time period.

As of the mid-1990s, there were no current thoughts on the eventual transition to the E/F version. But, in later years, it wouldn't be surprising if such an upgrade was made since through the years, the team has continuously striven to use the latest Navy fighter model.

A familiar sight at one of the many air shows across the country is a Blue Angel F/A-18 taking to the air. (US Navy Photo)

The smoke generated by the Blue Angel F/A-18s allows the crowd to follow the intricate maneuvers of the close-flying formations at high speeds. (US Navy Photo)

Though the frontline Navy fighter, the F/A-18 for Blue Angel use carries a smoke generator instead of a cannon. Here you can see the smoke just starting to push over the top of the upper wing surfaces. (US Navy Photo)

This long-range camera angle of the Blue Angels has the appearance of a multiple-image exposure, but these F/A-18s are flying extremely close together. (US Navy Photo)

Close formation flying at its best. To accomplish these tight formations it is necessary for four pilots in four aircraft to act as one. (US Navy Photo)

The tightness of the formation is vividly demonstrated by shadows of some planes cascading over others. This is exciting stuff. (US Navy Photo)

Ask any Blue Angel member about the capabilities of the Hornet to perform the team's intricate demonstrations, and you'll get an affirmative 'thumbs up.' The F/A-18 is awesome as a demonstration aircraft. The plane is highly maneuverable, powerful and fast, and a real crowd pleaser. From the ground point-of-view, the Hornet is also a very low-maintenance aircraft.

The formations the Blue Angels fly with their F/A-18s are considerably different from its rival Thunderbird team which uses the smaller F-16 as its demo aircraft. Blue Angel pilots

Look closely, this was not a collision, but a carefully choreographed Blue Angel maneuver. It illustrates the dogfighting maneuverability of the Hornet. (US Navy Photo)

One of the most exciting aspects of the Blue Angel performance is the head-on pass made by two Hornets. It's impossible for crowds on the ground to gage the vertical distance between the planes making it appear a lot closer than it really is. Note the planes are exactly on line separated only by vertical distance. (US Navy Photo)

A familiar site in St. Louis is seeing the hometown product, with the Navy Blue Angels, flying over the famous arch. (McDonnell Douglas Photo)

explained that the Blue Angels used a 'deeper stack' formation, with the Hornets being closer together, while the Thunderbirds usually flew higher altitude formations. Incidentally, the Blue Angel pilots do not use 'G' suits during their shows.

The redundancy of the Hornet pays big dividends in its role as a demonstration aircraft. The aircraft has a second completely-independent flight control system. Should anything happen to the electronic flight controls, the pilot has a mechanical back-up system with which to fly the plane. That's a pretty nice backup to have considering some of the weird attitudes in which these skilled pilots place their Hornets.

The Blue Angels are rated as one of the top flight demonstration teams in the world. And what better place to display the Navy's best fighter to the world than with the Blues??

Chapter 9:
F/A-18 Testbeds

A number of early production F/A-18s have found themselves accomplishing some interesting research and development non-combat missions, certainly far different than ever planned for the model. Following is a discussion of some of the major F/A-18 testbeds:

The F/A-18 EPAD Program

It might have seemed like fiction just a few years ago, but the concept of electrically-powered components leading to an all-electric aircraft could occur in the not-so-distant future.

The effort was coined the Electrically Powered Actuation Design(EPAD) validation program, and was a joint USAF, Navy, and NASA venture.

The F/A-18 was selected as the test aircraft for this program because it was a totally fly-by-wire aircraft, making it fairly easy to modify for a single actuator. More importantly, the performance requirements were significant step-ups in both response rates and power—the actual keys to electric actuation on fighter aircraft.

The initial flight testing for the F/A-18 EPAD program took place at NASA-Dryden at Edwards Air Force Base, California in the mid-1993 time period.

If successful, electric actuators could replace conventionally-powered actuators for control surfaces such as flaps and ailerons, and eventually eliminate the need for a central hydraulic system on an aircraft.

A major advantage of such a potential system is that it is environmentally friendly, with no hydraulic fluid to spill, dispose of, or store. Also, the future of this concept is not limited strictly to aircraft applications. Literally every piece of equipment that uses hydraulics could benefit from this technology.

The three-phased EPAD flight test program evaluated three types of electrical actuators. The program consisted of about two dozen missions per actuator, each mission lasting about one hour.

In initial tests, a 'smart actuator' replaced the conventional actuator powering the aileron on the left wing of the F/A-18 testbed.

The smart actuator was a conventionally-powered device using the central hydraulic systems, but the control electronics were mounted on the actuator itself. The device provided self-contained, fail-operate/fail-safe operation, as did the normal F/A-18 aileron actuator. The unit sensed the input from the flight control computer over a redundant optical bus and then electrically told the actuator to move. The actuator, though, moved the aileron by hydraulic power.

The F/A-18's flight control computer was not altered to accommodate the electrical actuator, but interface boxes

F/A-18s have served in a test role for many years. This is the NASA SRA(Systems Research Aircraft). This F/A-18B is based at NASA Dryden Flight Research Center and has been performing this test function since 1993. (NASA Photo)

The NASA SRA aircraft demonstrated successful operation of several fiber optic sensors including rudder position, rudder pedal position, landing edge flap position, nose wheel steering, and air pressure data. (NASA Photo)

The F/A-18 HARV vehicle started its test program in 1987 and was continuing into the mid-1990s. Clearly visible is the paddle activation system for deflecting engine exhaust. (NASA Photo)

A majority of the high angle-of-attack modifications were done on the rear portion of the F/A-18s fuselage as is clearly evident in this photo. (NASA Photo)

This photo shows the first flight of this F/A-18D testing the use of the Hornet in a night attack mode. The flight took place in May 1988. (McDonnell Douglas Photo)

This test aircraft, an F/A-18, is shown at Fallon in a test air-to-surface strike mission. Note the unique thunderbolt and 'Strike' on the vertical tail. (McDonnell Douglas Photo)

translated the flight messages into the language that the electronically controlled actuator could understand. Another unique aspect about the interface box was that it used fiber optics to connect with the actuator, one of very few fly-by-light technologies used in a testbed aircraft anywhere in the world.

F/A-18 SRA(Systems Research Aircraft) Testbed

The F/A-18 SRA has been involved in a number of NASA test programs, but its most important mission has been a series of tests that could result in lighter, more fuel-efficient aircraft concepts with more capable control and monitoring systems using a so-called Fly-By-Light concept.

The initial flight of the SRA testbed aircraft demonstrated successful opeation of several fiber optic sensors including rudder position, rudder pedal position, leading-edge flap po-

sition, nose wheel steering, total pressure, and air data temperature.

This particular effort was started in 1993 with the so-called Fiber-Optic Control System Integration(FOCSI) program. The purpose of the program was to examine fiber-optic engine controls and set the stage whereby a future transport aircraft could be fitted with partial fiber-optic or fly-by-light flight and engine control systems.

The FOCSI tests using the SRA plane had a goal of developing fiber-optic systems—small bundles of light-transmitting cable—that weigh less and take up less space than the copper wiring in today's aircraft.

The F/A-18 testbed aircraft was heavily instrumented, including sensors in (1) the left trailing and right leading edges, (2) the rudder and left stabilizer, and (3) on the engine power

The number six F/A-18A prototype participated in company test program called the High AOA program. This ceremony took place in 1979. (McDonnell Douglas Photo)

lever control. In addition, sensors were also added to determine aircraft pitch stick, rudder-pedal, and nose wheel positions.

Another phase of the program involved the fitting of a General Electric F404 powerplant with a number of optical sensors which monitored fan speed, inlet temperature, core speed, compressor inlet temperature, and turbine exhaust temperature.

In another later program, the SRA testbed aircraft was used in the More Electric Aircraft Program. This program had the goal of developing aircraft control systems where electric motors would be used instead of hydraulic systems to move control surfaces.

The potential benefits of this concept included 30-50 percent reduction in ground support equipment, five-to-nine per-

cent reduction in fuel consumption, and 600-to-1000 pounds reduction in take-off weight for commercial airliners.

With these, and other planned programs, the F/A-18 SRA aircraft should remain a busy and productive testbed aircraft throughout the 1990s.

The F/A-18 HARV Testbed with its dramatic black and gold paint scheme, the High Alpha Research Vehicle(HARV) F/A-18 testbed is the most recognizable of the F/A-18 testbeds.

The main purpose of this testbed is to improve performance at high angles of attack, the angle between the aircraft's body and wings relative to its actual flight path. However, flying at this attitude, problems are created when the airflow around the aircraft becomes separated from the airfoils. At high angles of attack, the forces generated by the

This F/A-18A is a NASA test aircraft in which a glycol-based liquid was released through very small holes around the nose to help researchers visualize airflow. This particular test shows the airflow pattern at about 30 degrees angle of attack. (NASA Photo)

aerodynamic surfaces-including lift provided by the wings-are greatly reduced. This flight attitude often results in insufficient lift to maintain altitude or control of the aircraft.

The HARV program produced technical data during that flight regime to validate computer analysis and wind tunnel research.

Successful validation of the data enable engineers and designers to understand the effectiveness of flight controls and airflow phenomena at high angles of attack.

The program began in 1987 with the first of three phases. The initial phase lasted for two and one-half years and consisted of 101 flights which flew at angles up to 55 degrees.

Phase two of the HARV program began in 1991, using a considerably modified airframe for the new test mission requirements. Three spoon-shaped paddle-like vanes, made of inconel steel, were mounted on the airframe around each engine exhaust. The devices deflected the jet exhaust to provide both pitch and yaw forces to enhance maneuverability at high angles of attack (AOA) when the aerodynamic controls were unusable or less effective than desired.

Also, the engines had their external exhaust nozzles removed to shorten the distance by two feet and the vanes had to be cant-levered. The unique thrust-vectoring modification precluded the test aircraft from being able to accomplish supersonic flight. The modification added about a ton to the craft's overall weight.

The new aircraft was able to achieve AOAs of up to 70 degrees, with this phase of the program being completed in late 1993.

During early 1994, the final phase of the program was undertaken, again with new airframe modifications. Additions included a pair of movable strakes which were mounted on both sides of the nose to provide enhanced yaw control at high AOAs. The four foot long, six-inch wide strakes were hinged on one side and mounted flush to the forward sides of the fuselage.

At low angles of attack, the strakes were folded flush against the aircraft skin, while they were extended at higher angles in order to interact with vortices generated along the nose. As a result, large side forces for enhanced control were produced effectively serving as a unique device to point the nose. Early research indicated that the strakes could be as effective at high angles of attack as rudders at the lower angles of attack.

Results of this testing in late 1995 indicated that the forebody controls are capable of providing the test aircraft with greatly-increased 'point and shoot' capability at high AOAs. The capability is increased when coupled with the thrust vectoring nozzles of the test plane.

AGM-154 Testing
During 1996, an F/A-18C served as a testbed aircraft for testing of the AGM-154 Joint Standoff Weapon(JSOW) at the Naval Air Weapons Station, China Lake, CA.

Typical missions consisted of low-speed launches of the 160-inch-long glide weapon. The JSOW is one of a number of precision guided standoff weapons that could be operationally fielded in the next decade. Obviously, the F/A-18 was an excellent platform to carry out this testing since the Hornet will be one of the carriers of the advanced weapon.

Chapter 10:
Future

The F/A-18 Hornet's future, just like the futures of other military items, will depend upon Department of Defense needs and funding. For example, the U.S. Navy currently is looking at modular Integrated Navigation and Electronic Warfare System (INEWS) technologies, developed originally for the Air Force's F-22, to enhance the Hornet's capabilities and survivability well into the 21st century but costs may preclude such a move. The notion of "sharing" technologies among service branches is not new but it could be the only financially viable way of bringing U.S. military fighter upgrades and developments into being.

Currently, there are at least two fighter programs which could affect the Hornet's 21st century use: the Air Force F-22 and the Navy-Air Force Joint Strike Fighter (JSF) program. The F-22 is to be the replacement for the F-15 Eagle and the JSF will replace Navy A-6s, Marine AV-8 Harriers, Marine Hornets, Air Force F-16 Falcons and British Harriers.

The F-22 grew out of the lengthy Advanced Tactical Fighter program and was in what the Air Force calls "engineering manufacturing development (EMD)" in the mid-1990s. This means that manufacturing processes are under development to ensure smooth program transition into production.

The biggest influence on the future of the Hornet is the USAF F-22, shown here in an early prototype flight in 1990. The F-22 is an extremely fast, long range fighter designed to replace the F-15 Eagle. Built by Lockheed-Martin, the F-22 is powered by two Pratt & Whitney F-119 engines. (Lockheed Photo)

During EMD, the program's two "demonstrator" aircraft continued to undergo extensive flight testing. In 1997, the first "true" F-22 prototype will begin tests and eventually will be joined by eight other prototypes.

Begun in the early 1980s, the F-22, according the Air Force, will combine low observable (or stealth characteristics) with "supercruise" (ability to fly supersonically for relatively long periods without using fuel-gulping afterburners—something that only the F/A-18C now can do) capability and a high degree of maneuverability. The F-22 also will be able to carry out air-to-surface missions.

Designed as a single-pilot fighter, the F-22 is built by Lockheed-Martin, Boeing and Pratt & Whitney. It is powered by two F119-PW-100 engines which feature thrust vectoring, a maneuverability and attitude enhancement in which the engine exhaust nozzles may be directed up, down, or side-to-side. It will carry a variety of modern ordnance including a typical weapons suite of two AIM-9 Sidewinders, four AIM-120 AMRAAMs, one 20mm Gatling gun and two 100 lb JDAMs (Joint Direct Attack Munition). The fighter is expected to be in operational status in 2003.

The JSF is so far a "paper" airplane designed with multiservice usage as a major goal. The Navy would use it as a replacement for its A-6 attack aircraft; the Marines: to replace both their AV-8 ASTOVL (Advanced Short Take-off and Vertical Landing) Harriers and their F-18s; and the Air Force: its massive F-16 fleet. Also Great Britain wants it to replace their AV-8s.

Using modern materials technologies such as composites and titanium alloys, the JSF ideally would be very light, compact and simple in design. As of the late 1990s, no design had been specified.

JSF grew out of a program called JAST, or Joint Advanced Strike Technology. This mid-nineties program identified non-platform-specific systems—such as radar, weapons, engines, avionics and others—which could be used by Air Force and Navy new aircraft developments in the next century. The Pentagon called for 80 percent commonality between aircraft.

The JAST program grew out of service needs: the Navy needed something to fill the void left by the cancelled A-12 (a highly-classified attack craft sporting a flying wing airframe reminiscent of a miniature B-2 bomber); the Marines needed close air support, high-survivability, and Harrier-like flight characteristics; and the Air Force needed a new fighter for the early 21st century since its many F-16s would near the end of their projected service lives at that time. The Air Force's Multi-Role Fighter study came and went producing no new fighter design.

Will the Department of Defense be able to afford both the F-22 and the JSF? The answer to that question could have a major effect upon the F/A-18's future. One might imagine also that the F/A-18 might have a major effect on the futures of the above-mentioned programs.

The reasons: the F/A-18 still has growth potential—in fact, the E/F in testing is an incredible 900 lbs below its weight maximum! Combat-proven in Desert Storm where they enjoyed a higher-than-ninety percent mission-capable rate, Hornets can carry an astonishing variety of air-to-air and air-to-surface weapons; Hornets have small radar cross-sections and the Cs are already supercruise capable (the F/A-18E/F now in flight testing is designed to be able to supercruise although that capability had not been demonstrated at the time of this writing) a design goal of F-22. Although there were studies in the 1980s on adapting the F-22 for carrier use, nothing came of them and the Hornet, from its inception, seems equally at home operating from carriers or runways. Lastly, F/A-18E/Fs are on the verge of production while production of the F-22 won't begin until at least 2003.

On the other hand, the F/A-18 doesn't have a top speed to match the F-22 and even with 480-gallon external fuel tanks the E/F won't match the F-22's range. However, the speeds and other capabilities of modern ordnance, the virtual disappearance of the long range threats of the Cold War Soviet Union, and the rise of stealth technologies may make these F-22 advantages over the F/A-18 a wash. One thing is clear however; the Air Force is committed to the F-22 and will find a way to afford it if at all possible (besides, the problems—including lawsuits—with cancelling the A-12 program are fresh in the memories of Department of Defense officials).

It's difficult to assess any JSF impact upon the F/A-18 since it barely is into its infancy, however JSF's ASTOVL requirements seem to point the JSF in a completely different direction than that of the Hornet. Despite the fact that the JSF is the newest proposed fighter and potentially has much to offer, its "infancy" makes it vulnerable to cancellation since so few resources—relatively speaking—have been spent on it.

A most interesting future for the F/A-18 might occur if the JSF is cancelled and the F-22 is continued. The 21st century Air Force still will need to replace its nearly 1600, by-then-aging F-16s; the F/A-18E/F will be in full production; and the more aircraft ordered, the lower the per-unit cost would be. What an irony it would be if the Air Force became interested in an aircraft whose predecessor it rejected back in the 1970s!

Whether or not the F-22 reaches production or the JSF goes into development, for the future, the Navy will depend to a great degree upon its F/A-18. Some sources even speculate that the Hornet eventually will replace all the Navy's fighter aircraft with carrier mixes of F/A-18Cs and E/Fs.

Weapons and the ability to carry them will allow the Hornet to remain a daunting fighter well into the next century. The Hornet will carry new missiles including air-to-air weapons such as the AIM-120 AMRAAM, which can locate and track targets beyond visual range and attack them and the AIM-9X which can be fired at targets to the front, sides or rear of the platform fighter. New air-to-surface weapons include the latest block Harpoon over-the-horizon, radar-guided, anti-ship missile having a range of more than 67 nautical miles; the SLAM (Stand Off Land Attack Missile), an infrared-guided and upgraded variant of the Harpoon designed to attack land targets such as buildings up to 50-plus nautical miles away; the SLAM-ER (Expanded Response) which will feature dramatic upgrades to the SLAM's guidance, controls and effective range; and the Navy/USAF AGM-154 JSOW (Joint Stand-off Weapon), a precision-guided glide bomb which has a range of 15 to 40 nautical miles (to enter U.S. and allies' inventories by 1999). The E/F will be able to carry virtually any fighter-borne weapon or ordnance in the Navy's inventory.

It's likely that several foreign nations will depend upon the Hornet as well. In fact, the F/A-18 is one of the only exportable fighters under procurement throughout the 1990s. Another is the cheaper F-16; McDonnell Douglas reportedly is exploring lower cost F/A-18 variants to compete with the F-16 in foreign military sales.

Reasonable projections of future foreign purchases include some of the original Hornet buyers such as Canada looking into purchasing E/F Hornets. There also is interest from other countries such as Hungary, the Czech Republic, Poland and the Philippines concerning Hornet buys. Reportedly, even France gave the Hornet some consideration before going with one of its own.

Foreign military buys are similar to domestic buys in that both types depend upon needs and funds. Each buyer wants to get as much for his money as he can and because the F/A-18 is relatively new, dependable, combat-proven, has growth potential, is air-to-air and air-to-surface capable, and has a reasonable price tag, the F/A-18 Hornet makes a good purchase.

It seems safe to assume that the F/A-18 Hornet will be around for many years to come.

Appendix:
USMC F/A-18 Squadrons(1996 Time Period)

Marine Corps Air Station Beaufort, SC:

VMFA-115 F/A-18A   Iwakuni, Japan Rotation #1
VMFA-122   "   "   "   "   "
VMFA-451   "   "   "   "   " ", Deact 1997
VMFA-224 F/A-18D   Aviano, Italy Rotation
VMFA-332   "   "   "   "
VMFA-533   "   "   "   "
VMFA-251 F/A-18C   USN Aircraft Carrier Rotation
VMFA-312   "   "   "   "   "

Marine Corps Air Station El Toro, CA:

VMFAT-101 F/A-18(A-D) Provides initial fleet replacement

Naval Air Station Miramir, CA:

VMFA-232 F/A-18C   Iwakuni, Japan Rotation #1
VMFA-235   "   "   "   "   " , Deact 1996
VMFA-121 F/A-18D   "   "   "   #2
VMFA-225   "   "   "   "   "
VMFA-242   "   "   "   "   "
VMFA-314 F/A-18C   USN Aircraft Carrier Rotation
VMFA-323   "   "   "   "   "

Marine Corps Air Station, Iwakuni, Japan

VMFA-212 F/A-18C   Iwakuni, Japan on perm. basis

Naval Air Station, Cecil Field, Florida:

VMFA-142 F/A-18A

Naval Air Station, Miramir, CA:

VMFA-134 F/A-18A

Naval Air Station, Fort Worth, Texas:

VMFA-112 F/A-18A

Andrews Air Force Base:

VMFA-321 F/A-18A

US Navy F/A-18 Squadrons(1996 Time Period)

NAF Atsugi, Japan:
VFA-27   F/A-18C
VFA-192   F/A-18C
VFA-195   F/A-18C

NAS Cecil Field, FL

VFA-15	F/A-18C	
VFA-37	F/A-18C	
VFA-81	F/A-18C	
VFA-82	F/A-18C	
VFA-83	F/A-18C	
VFA-87	F/A-18C	
VFA-105	F/A-18C	
VFA-106	F/A-18A/B/C/D	Fleet Readiness, Training
VFA-131	F/A-18C	
VFA-137	F/A-18C	

NAS Lemoore, CA

VFA-22	F/A-18C	
VFA-25	F/A-18C	
VFA-27	F/A-18C	
VFA-94	F/A-18C	
VFA-97	F/A-18A	
VFA-113	F/A-18C	
VFA-125	F/A-18A/B/C/D	Fleet Readiness, Training
VFA-146	F/A-18C	
VFA-147	F/A-18C	
VFA-151	F/A-18C	

US Navy Reserve

VFA-203	F/A-18A	Cecil Field, FL
VFA-204	F/A-18A	NAS New Orleans, LA

Also from the publisher

LOCKHEED F-117 NIGHTHAWK
An Illustrated History of the Stealth Fighter

Bill Holder & Mike Wallace

The F-117 was probably the most secret aircraft ever developed. The Stealth technology upon which the plane was based made it unique in its appearance. With its stark black appearance and wispy configuration, the plane was a strange departure from the sleek supersonic fighters of the period. This new book covers the technical and operational aspects of the Nighthawk from its initial use over Panama through its shining moment during Operation Desert Storm. Bill Holder and Mike Wallace are also the authors of *McDonnell-Douglas F-15 Eagle: A Photo Chronicle*. Bill Holder is also co-author, with Steve Markman, of *One-of-A-Kind Research Aircraft: A History of In-Flight Simulators, Testbeds & Prototypes* (both titles are available from Schiffer Publishing Ltd.).

Size: 8 1/2" x 11" over 120 color & b/w photographs
64 pages, soft cover
ISBN: 0-7643-0067-9 $19.95
Available October

McDONNELL-DOUGLAS F-15 EAGLE: A PHOTO CHRONICLE

Bill Holder & Mike Wallace

Photo chronicle covers the F-15 Eagle from planning and development to its success in Operation Desert Storm and post-Desert Storm. All types are covered, including foreign – Israel, Japan and Saudi Arabia.

Size: 8 1/2" x 11" over 150 color & b/w photographs
88 pages, soft cover
ISBN: 0-88740-662-9 $19.95